WWW Motivation Mining:

Finding Treasures for Teaching Evaluation Skills Grades 1-6

**Marilyn P. Arnone
and
Ruth V. Small**

A Publication of THE BOOK REPORT & LIBRARY TALK
Professional Growth Series

Linworth Publishing, Inc.
Worthington, Ohio

This book is dedicated to
Joseph Arnone
and
Jean Birnbaum
for all their loving support and encouragement.

Library of Congress Cataloging-in-Publication Data

Published by Linworth Publishing, Inc.
480 East Wilson Bridge Road, Suite L
Worthington, Ohio 43085

Copyright©1999 by Linworth Publishing, Inc.

Series Information:
    From The Professional Growth Series

All rights reserved. Reproduction of this book in whole or in part is prohibited without permission of the publisher.

Some images © www.arttoday.com

ISBN 0-938865-88-9

5 4 3 2 1

Acknowledgements

We are grateful to several friends and advisors for their support during the writing of this book. They include Stephanie Mann for her friendship and invaluable assistance in transcribing countless pages of interviews; Tom Hardy for being a great sounding board and sparking ideas that later showed up in this manuscript; and Marilyn's business partner and friend, MariRae Dopke, for being tolerant of the many hours away from the office that were put into the writing of this book.

Many thanks to the five library media specialists of Central Bucks County, Pennsylvania, for piloting the newest version of *WebMAC Junior* with more than 500 elementary students. We are especially grateful to Melissa Yates who was the catalyst for that study. We also are indebted to all the educators who shared the stories that are included in this book; to our seminar participants and other educators who either tested or provided critical feedback on some of the first versions of our instruments; to Mike Eisenberg for writing the foreword to this book and its companion book; and to our publishers for their encouragement and support as we wrote the final manuscript.

Finally, we would like to thank our families for their continuing inspiration and support in all our endeavors.

Author Biographies

Marilyn P. Arnone, Ph.D., is a children's media consultant and producer who loves working with children. She has a unique interdisciplinary background, blending practical experience and an understanding of electronic and broadcast media with strong credentials in education. Marilyn is President, New Product Research and Development, of Creative Media Solutions, Inc., where her adventures have covered the gamut from researching and writing educational videos and multimedia for government and corporate clients to conducting a comprehensive formative evaluation for a nationally televised children's program. Her research interests have centered on exploring children's motivation (particularly curiosity) and learning in interactive multimedia environments. Marilyn received her master's degree in education from Harvard University and her doctorate in instructional design, development, and evaluation from Syracuse University.

Ruth V. Small, Ph.D., is Associate Professor and Director of the School Media Program at the School of Information Studies at Syracuse University. She holds master's degrees in education from Hunter College and library science from Syracuse University where she received her doctorate in instructional design, development, and evaluation. Ruth's teaching and research focus on applying motivation theories to a variety of information-based learning, work, and virtual environments. "Dr. Ruth," as she is affectionately known by her students, was voted 1996 "Professor of the Year" by the graduate students of her school at Syracuse. In 1997 she was awarded the AASL/Highsmith Research Award for her innovative research on the motivational strategies used by library media specialists when teaching information skills to students. She is a national and international consultant and speaker on motivation and evaluation.

Foreword

When Ruth Small and Marilyn Arnone asked me to write the foreword for this book, I was pleased to do so because I consider both Ruth and Marilyn good friends and colleagues. And frankly, I would have made some positive and flattering comments even if the book was just "okay." Marilyn and Ruth are two of the most creative people I know, and I would have been able to stress my personal experiences of working with both of them on research, teaching, and creative projects.

I think back to all the collaborative curriculum and program planning that I've done with Ruth at the School of Information Studies at Syracuse University as well as our joint "information-based education" research and work on the Gateway to Educational Materials (GEM) project. With Marilyn, I remember the energy and excitement of working on the ERIC video—particularly her "surprise" version—a *Star Wars* takeoff that perfectly communicated our message of a new, cutting-edge ERIC.

However, there's no need to dwell on past accomplishments because this new venture is highly impressive on its own. THIS IS IMPORTANT WORK!!

Today, our information-intensive world is fundamentally different than it was just five years ago. The World Wide Web has completely changed the way people of all ages find and use information. We truly are overloaded with information. That's why everyone agrees that students must learn to be discriminating users of information. It's not enough for students to simply find information. They must know that there are varying degrees of quality, and they must be skilled in evaluating information quality through the application of criteria.

And, while lots of people (including me) talked about the need to help students develop these essential skills, Marilyn and Ruth went ahead and did something about it. They created a complete approach-Motivation Mining-to help students learn to "mine" quality information on the Web. Based on sound theory, Motivation Mining offers practical and easy-to-use techniques and tools for students and teachers. The heart of the approach is a flexible tool called *WebMAC*—the *Web Site Motivational Analysis Checklist*, with versions for teachers and students at different levels. *WebMAC* can be used for teaching, lesson planning, and classroom-based research. But enough of me trying to explain Motivation Mining—Marilyn and Ruth do a far better job throughout this well-planned and well-executed book.

Evaluating information is central to every part of the information problem-solving process. For example, every stage in the *Big6* process requires students to be able to evaluate information: in defining the key elements of an information problem, deciding on an information seeking strategy, selecting keywords to locate sources, identifying relevant information in sources, combining information in a product, and evaluating effectiveness and efficiency. With Motivation Mining, we finally have direction and substance in how to go about helping students to learn these essential evaluation abilities. Well done, and thanks Marilyn and Ruth!

Mike Eisenberg
Seattle, Washington

Table of Contents

DEDICATION...
ACKNOWLEDGEMENTS... i
ABOUT THE AUTHORS... ii
FOREWORD.. iii
PREFACE... x

PART I: MOTIVATION MINING FOR INFORMATION LITERACY 1

Chapter One: Evaluation as a Critical Information Skill
    Mine Map.. 3
    Introduction... 4
    Chapter Objectives 4
    Evaluation and Information Literacy 4
    The Explosion of Educational Web Resources................. 6
    Evaluating Web Sites... 10
    Coming Up 12
    Highlights of Chapter One 14
    Minestorming.. 15

Chapter Two: Motivation Mining and the World Wide Web
    Mine Map.. 17
    Introduction... 18
    Chapter Objectives 18
    Motivation and Learning....................................... 18
    E-V Theory in Classroom Environments...................... 19
    E-V Theory in Electronic Environments...................... 20
    What Is Motivation Mining, and Why Is It Important? 21
    Teacher Judgments of Content Validity...................... 22
    Students' Perceptions of Motivational Quality 22
    And the Pivotal Factor: A Web Site's Motivational Attributes 23
    Putting It All Together 24
    Internet Gripes 24
    Web Sites That Have What It Takes 27
    Coming Up 29
    Highlights of Chapter Two 31
    Minestorming.. 32

PART I SELF-CHECK.. 33
SUGGESTED RESPONSES TO PART I SELF-CHECK.................. 35

Table of Contents continued

PART II: MINING TOOLS FOR A MOTIVATIONAL ASSESSMENT 37

Chapter Three: Using a Motivational Assessment Tool to Evaluate Web Resources
    Mine Map. 39
    Introduction. 40
    Chapter Objectives 40
    Existing Web Evaluation Instruments 40
    The Web Site Motivational Analysis Checklist. 42
    WebMAC Junior-2000 43
    WebMAC Middle. 44
    Other *WebMAC* Instruments. 45
    Development and Testing 45
    From the Original *WebMAC Junior* to the Present 46
    A Pilot Study In Pennsylvania 47
    Three Ways To Use Web Site Motivational Assessment 50
    Coming Up 54
    Highlights of Chapter Three. 54
    Minestorming 55

Chapter Four: Administering the Instrument
    Mine Map. 57
    Introduction. 58
    Chapter Objectives 58
    Setting the Stage. 58
    Providing an Overview of the Web Site 59
    Interacting with the Web Site. 59
    Giving Students Directions. 60
    You As the Model. 61
    Ours Is Not the Only Way 61
    Coming Up 62
    Highlights of Chapter Four. 62
    Minestorming 63

Chapter Five: *WebMAC Junior—2000*: The Instrument
    Mine Map. 65
    Introduction. 66
    Chapter Objectives 66
    WebMAC Junior-2000 67
    Coming Up 71

Table of Contents continued

    Highlights of Chapter Five 71
    Minestorming 72

Chapter Six: Scoring *WebMAC Junior—2000*
    Mine Map 73
    Introduction 74
    Chapter Objectives 74
    Scoring Individually and As a Class 74
    Plotting the Scores 77
    Coming Up 81
    Highlights of Chapter Six 81
    Minestorming 82

Chapter Seven: Interpreting Results
    Mine Map 83
    Introduction 84
    Chapter Objectives 84
    Explaining the Significance of the A and B Scores 84
    What Makes a Web Site Interesting and Valuable 85
    What Makes a Web Site Work Well and Enjoyable 85
    Demonstrating How the A and B Scores
        Contribute to an Overall Rating 86
    Coming Up 88
    Highlights of Chapter Seven 88
    Minestorming 89
PART II SELF CHECK 90
SUGGESTED RESPONSES TO PART II SELF-CHECK 91

PART III: PANNING FOR WEB GOLD: MAKING MOTIVATION MINING WORK FOR YOU 93

Chapter Eight: A Treasure Chest of Ideas from Educators
    Mine Map 95
    Introduction 96
    Chapter Objectives 96
    Gems and Nuggets from the "MasterMines" 96
    The "Awesome Web Site" Award (*AWA*rd) 110
    Coming Up 111
    Highlights of Chapter Eight 111
    Minestorming 112

Table of Contents continued

Chapter Nine: Other Great Ideas for Using the *WebMAC* Instruments
    Mine Map 113
    Introduction 114
    Chapter Objectives. 114
    More Gems and Nuggets from the "MasterMines" 114
    The *WebMAC* Instruments for Lesson Planning. 114
    The *WebMAC* Instruments for Research and Design. 116
    Coming Up 120
    Highlights of Chapter Nine. 120
    Minestorming. 121

Chapter Ten: Motivation Mining into the Future
    Mine Map. 123
    Introduction 124
    Chapter Objectives 124
    Information Skills for the 21st Century. 124
    Final Thoughts. 125
    Coming Up 126
    Highlights of Chapter Ten. 126
    Minestorming 127

PART IV: SHARING THE WEALTH. 129

Chapter Eleven: A Workshop for Educators
    Mine Map. 131
    Introduction. 132
    Chapter Objectives 132
    Materials 132
    Workshop Outline 132
    Overhead Transparency Masters 135
    Handouts 152
    Certificate of Achievement 152
    Coming Up 157
    Highlights of Chapter Eleven 157
    Minestorming 158

Chapter Twelve: Teaching Students to Use *WebMAC Junior—2000*
    Mine Map. 159
    Introduction. 160
    Chapter Objectives 160

Table of Contents continued

Materials 160
Outline for Integrating Overheads 160
Overhead Transparency Masters 162
The *AWA*rd Nomination Form 177
Coming Up 178
Highlights of Chapter Twelve 178
Minestorming 179

BIBLIOGRAPHY 181
APPENDICES 185
    Appendix A: *Content Validity Checklist* 187
    Appendix B: Lesson Plans 191
    Appendix C: *WebMAC Middle* 211
    Appendix D: *WebMAC Junior Long Form* 221
    Appendix E: *Web Site Investigator* 233

INDEX 239

Preface

Today's students are using the World Wide Web for everything from research projects to simply surfing for stimulation and fun. As they prepare to be information literate citizens for the 21st century, we must help them learn to evaluate the wide range of information resources they will encounter. This book uses a "mining" analogy that suits our call to dig up Web treasures that will help motivate our young learners' quests for knowledge. We hope this book will provide you with some tools and ideas you can use to help students *mine* quality Web sites and distinguish Web "gold" from worthless pyrite (better known as "fool's gold"). Let's start right out with a definition of *Motivation Mining*, although it will be defined again later in the book. We define motivation mining the Web as the identification and extraction of Web resources that have the potential to enhance student learning by meeting important motivational criteria. Those motivational criteria are at the heart of this book.

Primarily, this book was designed for elementary and middle school teachers, library media specialists (LMSs), and teacher/LMS teams who are enthusiastic about finding new ways to excite students about learning critical information literacy skills. The purpose of the book is twofold: (1) it provides educators with practical, easy-to-use ways of applying motivational assessment techniques when selecting Web sites for inclusion in their lessons, and (2) it offers concrete examples (from us and many of your colleagues) of how to use Web evaluation with young learners. We share real-life stories and practical, easy-to-use strategies from elementary and middle school educators in their own words.

The book should also be useful to teachers and other educators who are developing school home pages and to those who are involved in or planning to conduct practical research on the effectiveness of Web sites. It describes and includes an innovative Web evaluation tool, developed specifically for use by elementary and lower middle school students to provide hands-on experience in evaluating the strengths and weaknesses of World Wide Web sites. The instrument is described in the context of teaching evaluation skills as part of a larger information literacy program for elementary students. It is one of the few instruments in which the children themselves are the evaluators. The book also includes an instrument that is appropriate for middle school children or children in the upper elementary grades. A companion book has been developed for high school educators, and it emphasizes ideas and examples selected specifically for an older audience.

This book uses a workbook format and is organized into four major parts. Each part contains several chapters as briefly described below. At the end of each chapter, we provide "Chapter Highlights" (a review of key points) and a "Minestorming" (individual brain-storming, with a "mining twist") page for the reader to record any original thoughts and ideas stimulated by reading that chapter. Because the book's theme is "Motivation Mining," we use a mining theme throughout.

Part I: Motivation Mining for Information Literacy focuses on the relationships among information literacy, motivation, and the evaluation of Web resources. It contains the following chapters:

Chapter One: Evaluation as a Critical Information Skill reviews some well-known information problem-solving models designed for use with students, describes the scope of Internet-based resources and services and the challenge of evaluating them, and discusses teaching and learning opportunities using Web resources.

Chapter Two: Motivation Mining and the World Wide Web explores some general motivation concepts and applies them to the Web. It then introduces the concept of *Motivation Mining* in the context of evaluating electronic resources. The theoretical foundation for the *WebMAC Junior–2000©* and *WebMAC Middle©* motivational assessment tools provided in future chapters is presented.

Part II: Mining Tools for Motivational Assessment includes *WebMAC Junior–2000*, the Web evaluation instrument designed for use by students from grades 1-4. Complete administration directions and scoring forms are also provided. Additionally, a more sophisticated middle school instrument is discussed and provided in the Appendixes as well as a longer version of *WebMAC Junior–2000*, which may be helpful to Web site designers and practical researchers. Part II contains the following chapters:

Chapter Three: Using a Motivational Assessment Tool to Evaluate Web Resources describes several existing evaluation instruments, introduces the *Web site Motivational Analysis Checklist (WebMAC)* instrument designed for evaluators in elementary school, and discusses its development and testing. Finally, this chapter looks at several ways educators can use motivational assessment with World Wide Web sites.

Chapter Four: Administering the Instrument provides detailed directions for instructing students on the use of the instrument along with suggestions of ways to vary administration.

Chapter Five: WebMAC Junior–2000: The Instrument is the reproducible instrument itself.

Chapter Six: Scoring the WebMAC Junior–2000 includes all forms for scoring the instrument, including the scoring key, reproducible student scoring sheet, class tally, and plotting grids.

Chapter Seven: Interpreting Results discusses how to explain the meaning of scores to students.

Part III: Panning for Web Gold: Making Motivation Mining Work for You provides an abundance of lesson plan ideas and examples submitted by educators for using and integrating the *WebMAC* instruments into elementary and middle school curriculums. Additional ideas from the authors are included. Part III contains the following chapters:

Chapter Eight: A Treasure Chest of Ideas from Educators includes stories from elementary and middle school practitioners relating how they are using the *WebMAC* instruments to teach evaluation skills and offers insights into successful motivational strategies that they have added to projects and assignments.

Chapter Nine: Other Great Ideas for Using the WebMAC Instruments discusses ways to use the instrument for planning lessons, conducting educational research, and designing new Web sites.

Chapter Ten: Motivation Mining into the Future provides our final thoughts on *motivation mining* for developing information literate citizens for the 21st century.

Part IV: Sharing the Wealth provides materials for offering inservice professional workshops and lessons for students. Part IV contains the following chapters:

Chapter Eleven: Workshop for Educators includes a workshop outline, reproducible overhead masters and handouts, and a certificate of achievement for teaching your colleagues how to use *WebMAC Junior–2000* with their students.

Chapter Twelve: Teaching Students to Use WebMAC Junior–2000 includes a content outline and reproducible overhead masters for teaching students how to use *WebMAC Junior–2000*.

Appendices

- *Appendix A: Content Validity Checklist* includes a quick checklist for educators when evaluating a Web site's content.
- *Appendix B: Lesson Plans* includes three complete lesson plans used to teach the lessons described in Chapter Eight.
- *Appendix C: WebMAC Middle* includes the reproducible *WebMAC Middle* designed for students in grades 5-8, but which may be appropriate for upper elementary school students. It also includes the *WebMAC Middle* student scoring sheet, score key, plotting grids and class tally.
- *Appendix D: WebMAC Junior Long Form* includes the reproducible Long Form instrument designed for students in elementary school; it contains eight more items than *WebMAC Junior–2000*. Also included are the *WebMAC Junior Long Form* student scoring sheet, score key, plotting grids, and class tally.
- *Appendix E: Web Site Investigator* includes a reproducible 12-item questionnaire adapted from *WebMAC Junior–2000*. This brief instrument does not include scoring grids and is appropriate for very young children or as an introduction to Web site evaluation.

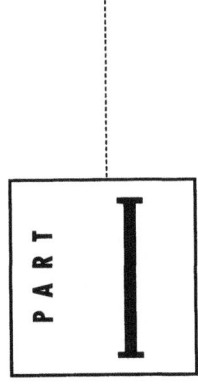

Motivation Mining for Information Literacy

Evaluation As a Critical Information Skill

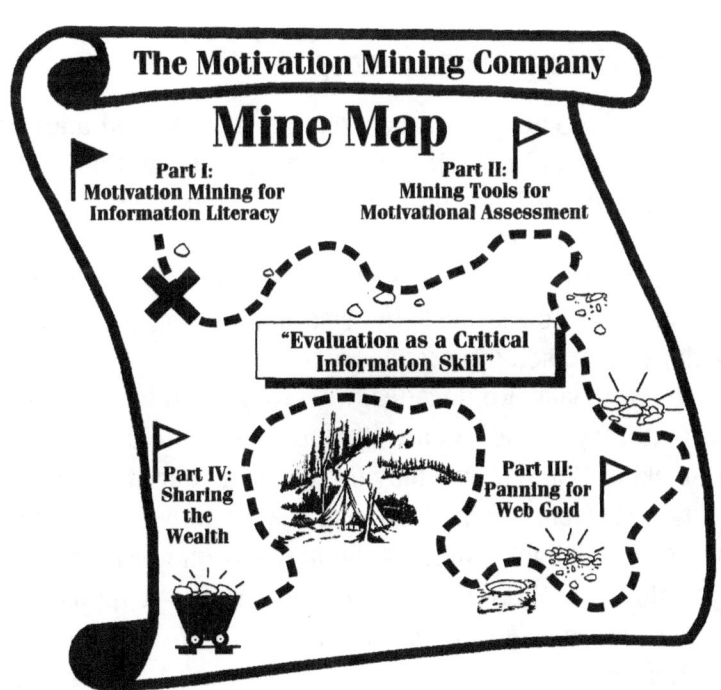

Introduction

Welcome to mining country—*motivation mining*, that is! We hope you will join us in prospecting for Web gold, the kind of Web sites that have the potential to engage learners and enhance learning. We will discuss more about the concept of *motivation mining* and how it applies to evaluating World Wide Web resources in Chapter Two. And in Part II, we'll provide the mining tools you'll need to get underway in your own mining endeavors. Before we stake out that territory, however, Chapter One will first address evaluation in general as a vitally important information skill. Then, we will review the wide variety of resources and services available to educators and students on the Internet and the challenge of evaluating them.

Chapter Objectives

When you've completed Chapter One, you will be able to:
▶ understand the role of evaluation in an information literacy context.
▶ describe several resources and services available to educators and students on the Internet and the challenge of evaluating them.
▶ understand the importance of evaluating Web resources for teaching and learning.

Evaluation and Information Literacy

Many of the readers of this book may have a good understanding of *information literacy* and experience in teaching information skills. As defined by a number of publications and organizations, information literacy generally refers to the ability to locate, evaluate, use, and present information in a variety of formats. Information literate students have been defined as "effective users of ideas and information."[1] Information literacy is a critical attribute of today's independent, self-directed learner.

During the past two decades, we have seen the development of several information literacy models, many of which designate a number of critical information skills. Some of you may be teaching your students the *Big6 Model of Information Problem-Solving*.[2] You will see a number of references to the *Big6 Model©* in this book. Some of you may use one or more other models such as Stripling and Pitts' *Research Process Model*,[3] Pappas and Tepe's *Pathways to Knowledge: Follett Information Skills Model*,[4] Yucht's *FLIP-IT* model,[5] or Kuhlthau's *Model of the Search Process*.[6] As you are aware, most models break information skills into general categories from task definition through evaluation. In our book, *Turning Kids on to Research: The Power of*

Motivation,[7] we synthesize common skills in existing models into eight general, critical evaluation skills pictured below. Evaluation is highlighted as one of these skills.

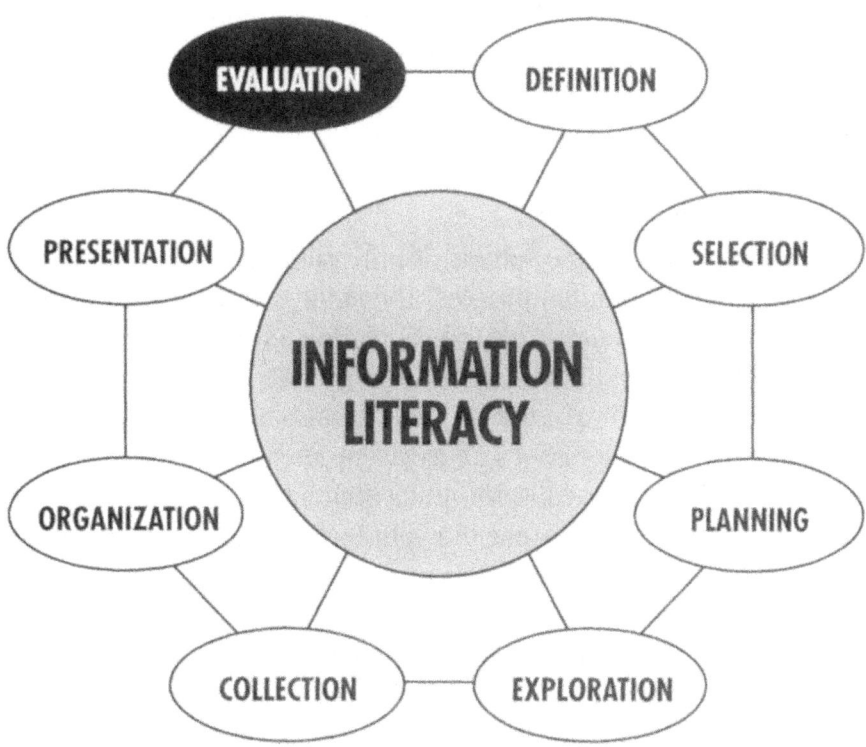

Benjamin Bloom, in his well-known *Taxonomy of Educational Objectives*, recognized evaluation as the highest form of learning.[8] It is only one but a very critical information skill associated with information literacy and is included in virtually every information literacy model. The new national standards for information literacy support its importance in its Standard 2: "The student who is information literate evaluates information critically and competently."[9]

As the amount of world knowledge continues to double about every three to five years,[10] the students of today must develop a critical evaluative perspective in order to discern accurate and credible information from that which is unreliable. Teaching young children how to evaluate information resources in a basic way is an important prerequisite to utilizing more advanced evaluation techniques. Michael Eisenberg and Robert Berkowitz have developed the widely used *Big6 Model of Information Problem Solving*, which includes six basic information skills that students need to master. These skills are task definition, information seeking strategies, location and access, use of information, synthesis, and evaluation. Each general skill is further broken down into two steps. Eisenberg and Berkowitz point out that while the *Big6* appears to be a step-by-step process, the steps actually can occur in a somewhat different order as long as all the skills are eventually mastered in time.

The steps outlined above, however, may be too complex initially for the youngest learners (e.g., kindergarten, first graders), so Eisenberg and Berkowitz proposed a simpler model for the early grades. This simpler model is called the *Super Three*, and it encompasses the essence of the *Big6*. They often use the *Super Three* before teaching the *Big6*. It includes:

▶ Beginning (Plan what you are going to do),
▶ Middle (Do it), and
▶ End (Review what you did).

While the *Super Three* sounds like the parts of a story, it is still based on the flow of the information process. The model can be used to explore both print and electronic resources. More information on the *Big6* can be found in several references listed at the end of this book. We mention the *Big6* in this book written primarily for elementary educators because it works so well with the younger learners. It also does an excellent job of addressing the evaluation component of information skills, including student evaluation of resources, the final product, and the process used to get there. As mentioned earlier, there are other widely used models that also emphasize an evaluative component. For example, Pappas and Tepe's *Pathways to Knowledge Model* (mentioned earlier) has an "interpretation" phase in which the student assesses the usefulness and personal relevance of each resource and its information. McKenzie's *Research Cycle Model*[11] recommends evaluating the quality of electronic information and information resources.

Now that we've discussed the importance of evaluation in general, let's begin to move closer to the focus of this book, Web-based resources, and eventually explore the evaluation of Web sites.

The Explosion of Educational Web Resources

The literature abounds with articles by and about educators who are using electronic resources in their teaching (e.g., for introducing or enriching content) and students who are using Internet resources to conduct research and complete assignments and other learning tasks. Kathy Tobiason,[12] librarian at the American School in Tokyo, Japan, collaborated with the third and fourth grade teachers in her school to identify, bookmark, and organize appropriate Internet sites, develop original student-created material for their elementary school home page, and link the two into "unit home pages." Barbara Seigel[13] developed an interdisciplinary social studies/language arts unit on inventions and technology. The ultimate goal for her fifth and sixth grade students was to create oral presentations and written reports to demonstrate their understanding of the invention process and the connections between historical events and the development of new technology. For their projects, students were required to use the Internet as a research tool. Linda C. Joseph, library media specialist in the Columbus, Ohio, public schools (and her alter ego, Cyberbee), regularly publishes articles in *Multimedia Schools* (and online at http://www.infotoday.com/MMSchools/MMStocs/MMScybertoc.html). Joseph's articles describe theme-related Web sites on popular topics (e.g., science fair projects, dinosaurs) for use in learning activities.

Within a few short years, the Internet has become a well-accepted information resource for teaching and learning. Some say it is even becoming *the* primary information source.[14] Mike Eisenberg contends that "today and in the future, the concept of Library should encompass the full range of information resources-electronic and print."[15]

It is unusual now for a school *not* to be connected to the Internet, and further encouraging its use in teaching. According to a national survey released in 1999, 89 percent of schools were connected to the Internet in 1998.[16] Those statistics will soar significantly by the time this book is even published. Steven Hackbarth describes three types of Web-based learning activities:

▶ Communications,
▶ Information retrieval, and
▶ Information sharing.[17]

The ability to evaluate Web site features such as guidance, feedback, content validity, author credibility, and navigation becomes critical in all of the above activities.

Web sites used for teaching and learning may contain anything ranging from information on a single topic to databases of text or images on one or more topics, and from lesson plans and single activities to unit plans, curriculum guides, and state and national standards mapping.

The *Ask-an-Expert* Services (sometimes called simply "Ask-A" services have become quite popular and include expert help on any number of subjects from science and math to more general help in researching possible citations for a project. The award-winning *AskERIC* service does a great job at the latter. It was started as an e-mail question-and-answer service for educators and parents. Any educational question is fair game from questions on block scheduling to the censorship of books. Within 48 hours, the information specialists, depending on your question, can provide anything from the addresses of useful Internet sites or listservs to the full text of related *ERIC Digests*. Today, *AskERIC* has expanded to include a Virtual Library of resources, including lesson plans and *InfoGuides*. If you have a question, you can e-mail it to *AskERIC* at askeric@ericir.syr.edu. There are also dozens of other "Ask-an-Expert" serv-

other "Ask-an-Expert" services that are useful to elementary educators and students for subject-specific questions. David Lankes and Abby Kasowitz provide a review and insight on a number of such sites.[18]

The potential Web resources that could be useful to educators are too numerous to list within the scope of this book, and there are already publications that do a good job of reviewing particular Web sites. However, several types of networked resources have been described by Ruth Small and Bernard Lee[19] and should at least be mentioned. They include:

▶ **Federal Government Sites.** There are a number of large databases of educational information provided by various government agencies and clearinghouses. For example, NASA's site (http://www.nasa.gov) contains all kinds of information about the universe and space travel for all ages. The Smithsonian Education Web site (http://educate.si.edu/lessons/start.html) gives upper elementary and middle school teachers and students access to primary sources, museum collections, and materials on subjects ranging from aeronautics to zoology.

▶ **State Government Sites.** A variety of state-based initiatives have funded the development of educational Web sites that provide a wide range of resources and services to the K-12 community. For example, North Carolina's Department of Public Education Web site features "Tried-n-True Dynamite Lesson Plans" (http://www.ofps.dpi.state.nc.us/OFPS/tc/TNT/index.html), a compilation of model lesson plans created by teachers, and for teachers, at all levels and linked to state education standards.

▶ **Commercial Sites**. A growing number of commercial Web sites are providing free or fee-based services and resources to the K-12 education community. For example, Microsoft's Encarta Online (http://encarta.msn.com/schoolhouse/lessons/default.asp) offers a collection of K-12 lesson plans organized by topics, ranging from fine arts to computers and information technology. Classroom Connect (http://www.classroom.net) offers a searchable database of K-12 educational products, links to lesson plans and other instructional materials, and an Internet searching guide.

▶ **Individual Sites.** A countless number of sites have been developed by single individuals and organizations to provide information and activities for teachers and students about a single topic or one or more particular subject areas. The Crayola Crayon Web site (http://www.crayola.com) is a colorful site that offers all kinds of art activities. Carol Hurst's Children's Literature Site (http://www.carolhurst.com) provides book reviews, classroom activities, and ideas for using literature within the curriculum. The Weather Dude (http://www.weatherdude.com) provides weather-related information and games.

▶ **Metasites**. There are also a number of Web sites that comprehensively organize other sites on specific subject areas or topics. Mike Tillman calls these "metasites."[20] For example, Math Forum (http://forum.swarthmore.edu/) organizes math resources by subject area for all grade levels. Kathy Schrock's Guide for Educators (http://www.capecod.net/schrockguide) provides a compilation of Internet sites organized by subject areas, materials to help educators understand basic Internet concepts, links to other Web sites, and tools for helping students and teachers evaluate Web sites. KidsConnect Favorite Sites (http://www.ala.org/ICONN/kcfavorites.html) provides a list of the favorite Web sites used by a group of "cybrarians."

▶ **The Gateway to Educational Materials** (GEM) (http://gateway.org) is perhaps the most comprehensive metasite available to educators. GEM provides educators with one-stop, any-stop access to a large range of education-related, Web-based collections that contain thousands of lesson plans, curriculum units, and other Internet-based educational resources. GEM allows users to search all of the collections within its membership by simultaneously using specific criteria (e.g., grade level, subject area, quality level) to conduct a more precise search and pinpoint the exact kinds of materials desired. This saves the time and effort it takes to search each of these collections individually. GEM encompasses both large collections, such as *AskERIC*'s Virtual Library and smaller collections of materials for teaching and learning, such as those of the National Council for Agricultural Education, DramaWest, Tramline Virtual Field Trips, and Computer Curriculum Corporation.

Not only are these types of resources useful when teaching subject-specific information, but they can also be valuable resources for teaching students the range of information skills. For example, when teaching *planning* strategies (deciding what types of resources will be used), your lesson can include "Ask-A" services where students seek information directly from experts in a particular field.

Educators are using any and all of these resources in their teaching (e.g., for introducing or enriching content), while students are using Internet resources to conduct research and complete assignments and other learning tasks. Kathy Finder and Donna Raleigh describe a framework for developing K-12 Web-based assignments tied to specific educational objectives and environments.[21] Leu et al. provide a number of strategies for effectively integrating the Internet into classroom teaching and learning, while incorporating stories from actual teachers who represent various subject areas.[22] Candace Boyer promotes the use of museum Web sites and other resources as social studies teaching resources.[23] Frederick and Jean Abel give examples of ways teachers can use Web sites and other Internet resources to integrate the disciplines of mathematics and social studies.[24]

Internet resources, then, can be useful to teach students subject-specific information as well as information skills. Yet, one hears very little about the criteria that educators use to select Web sites for their lessons. How can students know a quality Web site when they see one? With the abundance of available Web resources, one of the most critical information skills students will need is evaluation.

Evaluating Web Sites

"If it's on the Web, it must be OK to use in my research." That's the sentiment we've heard from so many students. One of the considerable challenges of educators today is to convince students otherwise. Without accountability on the part of those who develop Web sites, students' evaluation skills will be of prime importance. Tobias Rademann states "...there has not yet been any kind of quality-control mechanism implemented on the Web, which means that students would definitely have to be taught how to judge the reliability and the value of the various sources they come across..."[25] Others cite the importance of "digital literacy," that is, being able to understand and use information from a range of computerized resources.[26] Students require a "toolbox" of thinking and problem-solving skills to help them manage what they find. As Jamie McKenzie states, "the new information landscape requires literacy skills well beyond those needed in previous times, and learners soon find that digital sources are insufficient for many questions and topics."[27]

Unfortunately, the enormous increase of information resources on the Web has not ensured that Web developers will be accountable for the validity or quality of their Web sites. Therefore, it is the responsibility of both students and teachers to make judgements about the value of a particular site for their needs. Students need to know that it is not enough to simply retrieve the first Web site that their keyword search turns up and use that as the basis of their research. How do you impress upon students the importance of evaluating information resources?

One library media specialist we interviewed for this book, Gail Gilland, from Damascus (Virginia) Middle School used a poignant current event to demonstrate the importance of evaluating Web sites to her students. During a session she conducted in the library media center, she and her students discussed URLs, or Web addresses, and how sometimes they can be an instant clue as to whether a source might be an authority or not. The event she chose was the Columbine High School massacre in Littleton, Colorado, in April 1999. For several days, all over the country, students could scarcely concentrate on anything else. Since her students were already riveted on that subject, she created a learning opportunity around it that would result in her students truly grasping the importance of being able to critically evaluate information resources. This is how she described the discussion:

> "I asked my students, 'What if in your Civics class, you were all assigned to do a report on a dictator?' And then I pointed at one of the students and said, 'What if you were assigned to do a report on Hitler? Trust me, there are probably thousands of Web pages out there that would have something on that topic. What would you do if you got the list of hits, and before you even went to any of them, you looked at the URLs? And by looking at those, you could tell something about what it was. Had you gotten that young man's page (Colorado student gunman) on Hitler, would that be considered an authoritative page?... This is just an example right here that if you did a search on this subject, you just might have come up with this young man's Web page.'"

The students were engrossed in the discussion. As Gail and her students continued reflecting on the importance of evaluation, she taught them about domain names like .edu and .gov. Her lesson was a success; the students were likely to remember this one. Why? She was able to tap into two motivational strategies that work great: (1) capturing interest and (2) making the activity relevant. Gail explained, "It was right there in the news. It had their attention, and I was able to tie that in with what sometimes can be a boring thing—talking about Web addresses!"

Teachers and LMSs also need to use evaluative criteria in selecting Web resources to use in lesson planning. Reference/instruction librarians Jan Alexander and Marsha Ann Tate note that the evaluation of networked information resources, such as Web sites, requires a unique set of criteria and new, easy-to-use tools that encompass a broader concept of evaluation.[28]

COMING UP...

In Chapter Two, we discuss the concept of motivation and what we call motivation mining the Web. We also outline the critical factors for a successful Web site and offer a brief glimpse of a newly developed Web evaluation tool that encompasses a broader concept of Web site evaluation.

ENDNOTES

[1] American Association of School Librarians and Association for Educational Communications and Technology, *Information Power: Building Partnerships for Learning*. Chicago: American Library Association, 1998, p.6.

[2] M. B. Eisenberg, and R. E. Berkowitz, *Information Problem-Solving: The Big Six Skills Approach to Library & Information Skills Instruction*. Norwood, NJ: Ablex Publishing Corporation, 1990.

[3] B.K. Stripling and J. M. Pitts, *Brainstorms and Blueprints*. Englewood, CO: Libraries Unlimited, 1988.

[4] M.L. Pappas and A. E. Tepe, "Follett Information Skills Model." In *Teaching Electronic Information Skills*. McHenry, IL: Follett Software Company, 1995.

[5] A. Yucht, *FLIP IT! An Information Skills Strategy for Student Researchers*. Linworth Publishing, Inc. 1997.

[6] C. Kuhlthau, "Implementing a Process Approach to Information Skills: A Study Identifying Indicators of Success in Library Media Programs." *School Library Media Quarterly*, 22 (1), 1993, pp.11-18.

[7] R.V. Small and M. P. Arnone, *Turning Kids on to Research: The Power of Motivation*, Libraries Unlimited, 1999.

[8] B.S. Bloom et. al, *Handbook on Formative and Summative Evaluation of Student Learning*. New York: McGraw-Hill, 1971.

[9] American Association of School Librarians and Association for Educational Communications and Technology, p. 8.

[10] T. Rademann. *Information Unlimited: Employing Internet Resources in Education* http://www.isoc.org/inet97/proceedings/D3/D3_1.HTM, 1997.

[11] J. McKenzie, "Making WEB Meaning." *Educational Leadership*, 54 (3), 1996, pp. 30-32.

[12] K. Tobiason, "Tailoring the Internet to Primary Classrooms." *Technology Connections*, April 1997, pp. 8-9.

[13] B. Seigel, "Eureka! Discovering Inventions and Technology." *Technology Connection*. October 1997, pp. 18-19.

[14] Rademann, 1997.

[15] M. B. Eisenberg, "Take the Internet Challenge: Using Technology in Context." *The Book Report, 15* (Sept/Oct 1996) p. Supp. 5-7 [Spec. suppl.], September 1996, p.5.

[16] "Public Schools with Internet Access Make Significant Strides in 1998." *Educational Technology News, 16* (5). Business Publishers, Inc., March 3, 1999, p.34.

[17] S. Hackbarth, "Web-Based Learning in the Context of K-12 Schooling." In *Educational Media and Technology Yearbook, 22*, 1997, pp.109-131.

[18] R. D. Lankes and A. S. Kasowitz, *AskA Starter Kit: How to Build and Maintain Digital Reference* Services. Syracuse, NY: ERIC Clearinghouse on Information & Technology, 1998.

[19] R. V. Small and B. Lee, "Web-Based Resources for K-12 Instructional Planning." In R. M. Branch and M. A. Fitzgerald (Eds.), *Educational Media and Technology Yearbook, 24*, 1999, pp. 58-63.

[20] M. Tillman, *Education Metasites*. ERIC Clearinghouse on Information & Technology, 1998. (ERIC Document Reproduction Service No. ED 423877)

[21] K. Finder and D. Raleigh, *Establishing a Framework Useful for Developing Web-Based Assignments in K-12 Education*, 1998. (ED421099) Published in Proceedings In Site 98: Society for Information Technology & Teacher Education International Conference, Washington D.C.

[22] D. J. Leu, D. D. Leu and K. R. Leu, *Teaching with the Internet: Lessons from the Classroom*. Christopher-Gordon Publishers, 1999.

[23] C.L. Boyer, "Using Museum Resources in the K-12 Social Studies Curriculum." *ERIC Digest*. Bloomington, IN: ERIC Clearinghouse for Social Studies/Social Science Education, 1996. (ED412174)

[24] F.J. Abel and J. P. Abel, *Integrating Mathematics and Social Studies: Activities Based on Internet Resources*. Paper presented at the Annual Meeting of Teachers of Mathematics, Helena, MT, October 18, 1996.

[25] Rademann, p.7.

[26] P. Gilster, *Digital Literacy*. New York: Wiley, 1997.

[27] McKenzie, 1996.

[28] J. Alexander and M. Tate, "Teaching Web Evaluation: Meeting the Challenge." *Internet Trend Watch for Libraries*, 3 (2). Librarians and Educators Online, 1998.

HIGHLIGHTS of Chapter One

In Chapter One, we discussed evaluation as an integral aspect of information literacy. It is now designated as a critical thinking skill in the new national standards of information literacy. Several information literacy models were mentioned with emphasis on the *Big6* since this model particularly addresses very young students. All information literacy models include evaluation as a critical component. We also discussed the availability of a number of different Internet resources for teaching and learning including Ask-an-Expert Services, federal and state government sites, commercial, and individual sites. Web-based learning activities encompass communications, information retrieval, and information sharing. The ability of students to judge the content and credibility of Internet resources is becoming increasingly important as the amount of information continues to build at a rapid pace. Presently, there is no quality control of the Internet, and therefore teachers and students are left on their own to judge the merits of its contributors.

 **MINESTORMING**

As you were reading, did you think of any new ways you might use Web resources in a future lesson plan? Jot down your ideas now while they are fresh in your mind. Then come back later and flush them out when you have read more. By the way, "minestorming" is our word for individual brainstorming in the motivation mining context.

_____
_____
_____
_____
_____
_____
_____
_____
_____

Motivation Mining and the World Wide Web

Introduction

With the proliferation of educational Web sites in the last few years, educators have felt compelled to begin incorporating World Wide Web resources into their lesson plans. Many teachers and library media specialists have told us about how well-prepared they are, how they present their lessons in an enthusiastic manner, and how they generally use what are considered to be excellent teaching strategies, yet still feel a particular lesson is not effective in terms of their objectives. As a teacher, you may shine, but we all know that a weak link (no pun intended) can result in even the best-laid plans going awry. So, perhaps, there is another reason for the less than excellent outcomes. That reason often lies in the *motivational quality* of the Web site. In this chapter, we discuss motivation and its importance for student achievement and introduce the concept of *Motivation Mining*.

Chapter Objectives

When you've completed Chapter 2, you will be able to:
▶ describe the role of motivation in learning.
▶ explain the concept of *Motivation Mining*.
▶ describe several ways in which motivation mining can be useful.
▶ describe the relationship between teacher judgments, student perceptions, and Web site attributes in successful Web-based instruction.
▶ understand the role of functionality in the context of motivational quality.
▶ understand how Web site attributes and obstacles can affect motivation.

Motivation and Learning

Motivation is said to answer the "why" of behavior. That is, why does someone spend more time or effort on one thing as opposed to another? Sometimes, it is because there is an external reward such as an allowance, a grade, or an award. Other times, it is because just participating in the activity or learning challenge brings satisfaction and pleasure. The latter refers to *intrinsic* motivation or motivation that comes from within. Motivation is important because research indicates that ability (possessing needed knowledge and skills) does not account for all the variation in student achievement. At least some of that variation is due to the student's motivation. So, motivation is a critical component of learning and especially of the desire for life-long, self-directed learning. In an information literacy context, Carol Kuhlthau asserts, "One of the key considerations in designing a research task is motivation of students."[1] Throughout this book, we'll be discussing a variety of elements and strategies that affect motivation, focusing particularly on the Internet.

One of the most widely known and applied motivation theories is the Expectancy-Value (E-V) Theory.[2] This theory has been described as "one of the most promising models of individual motivation."[3] E-V theory specifies that the amount and quality of a person's effort in a given task or activity depends on two critical prerequisites—the *perceived value of the task and an expectation that he or she can be successful in achieving that task*. Therefore, people will not voluntarily put forth effort for a task that holds little or no personal value. Nor will people willingly participate in an activity in which they believe that no matter how hard they try, they are incapable of succeeding. Although it was originally developed to explain motivation in the workplace, recently researchers have found that E-V theory may have appropriate applications in classroom and electronic environments.

E-V Theory in Classroom Environments

Hansen describes four potential student responses to assigned tasks or activities in the context of E-V Theory.[4] If the student values a task *and* has high expectations for success, *engagement* in the activity results (Response 1). However, if the student values the activity but believes there is little or no chance for success, *dissembling* occurs (Response 2). Jere Brophy describes dissembling in this way: "[Students] would like to complete the task successfully, but are uncertain of what to do, how to do it, or whether they can do it. [This causes them to] pretend to understand, make excuses, deny their difficulties, or engage in other behavior..."[5] On the other hand, if the student has high success expectations but doesn't care about it, the result is evasion; that is, doing the minimum required (Response 3). Finally, if the student neither values the activity nor has high success expectations, the result is often complete *rejection*, a refusal to participate and withdrawal from the activity (Response 4).

You have probably observed or experienced all of these responses in students at one time or another. Some educational theorists have used Expectancy-Value Theory to develop strategies to maximize Response 1 and avoid or minimize Responses 2, 3, and 4. Brophy maintains that much of the research on student motivation may be organized within E-V Theory. He asserts that teachers must (1) help students appreciate the value of learning tasks or activities and (2) make sure that, with a reasonable amount of effort, students can successfully complete these tasks or activities.[6]

In his work on motivating adult learners, Raymond Wlodkowski states, "Adults feel much better when they have successfully learned something they wanted to learn as well as something they value."[7] He also describes a number of instructional strategies that may be used to increase a learner's expectancy for success. He maintains, "Demonstrating clearly that the learning task is concretely possible to achieve is a significant positive influence on the learner's attitude toward learning."[8] These important strategies also apply to children's learning.

One of the most comprehensive applications of E-V theory in education is John Keller's ARCS Model of Motivational Design.[9] The ARCS Model specifies four essential factors of motivating instruction: *Attention, Relevance, Confidence, and Satisfaction*. Keller maintains that gaining and maintaining *Attention* and providing *Relevant* resources and activities will increase a student's perceived *Value* of a learning task. Furthermore, providing useful feedback and encouragement, designing instructional resources and activities that are on the appropriate level of challenge to increase student *Confidence*, and rewarding progress toward achievement of learning goals to foster *Satisfaction* will fortify a student's *Expectation for Success* in a learning task.

E-V Theory in Electronic Environments

Recently, researchers have found that E-V Theory can also be used to explain people's behavior in electronic environments. For example, researchers found that E-V Theory was a significant predictor of motivation to use an expert system. They found that the theory was useful early in the design phase to assess the user's intention to use the expert system, which in turn would help guide decisions about the design.[10] Other researchers have found E-V Theory to be valuable in investigating managers' motivation to voluntarily use a computer-based decision support system. They maintain "that users not only need to value potential system-related outcomes, but must also reasonably expect to experience these outcomes as a result of system use."[11]

We believe E-V theory can be effectively applied to a Web environment, as well.[12] Under E-V theory, the user must (1) perceive the Web site as containing relevant and useful information presented in an interesting manner and (2) believe that he or she can successfully navigate the Web site and gain access to needed information. E-V theory also appears to be highly useful for developing evaluation criteria that identify which features motivate a person to visit, explore, and revisit a Web site.

In fact, *Value* and *Expectation for Success* have a multiplicative function. That is, both factors must be strong in order for the motivational quality of a Web site to be high. If either factor is absent (or "zero"), then the result is an ineffective Web site because the student will not be motivated to stay and explore or return at another time. Let's think of it in mathematical terms:

Value		Expectation for Success		
1	X	0	=	0
0	X	1	=	0
1	X	1	=	SUCCESS!

What Is Motivation Mining, and Why Is It Important?

Recently, much attention has been focused on what is termed "data mining" the Web, or what we broadly defined as choosing and extracting appropriate, credible, and useful information from the Web. Data mining, in a stricter sense, often involves discovering new or hidden patterns and trends in large databases of information. Sometimes, secret treasures can be found within the vast amounts of information. Uncovering such riches of information can translate into big bucks for the companies that do that research and make use of it. Data mining the Web focuses on finding useful data on the Web.

By the same token, there are wonderful treasures to enhance teaching and learning can be found on the Web. You can discover these riches by "Motivation Mining" the Web.[13] We define motivation mining the Web as the identification and extraction of Web resources that have the potential to enhance student learning by meeting important motivational criteria. These resources provide the content required to complete the task *and* engage and satisfy the Web site user. Motivation mining, therefore, focuses on finding the highest quality Web sites for teaching and learning.

Unfortunately, when using the Web, there are many opportunities for students to have discouraging experiences. If the research on motivation suggests that students must also be motivated in order to learn, then it is not enough that educators only judge the appropriateness and authenticity of the content of a specific Web site to guarantee a successful teaching and learning episode. We must *also* be able to determine the motivational aspects for student learning (this includes student judgments of content, which affect motivation). Therefore, when measuring the success potential of educational Web resources for teaching, there are three important considerations:

(1) *Teacher judgments* based on expertise in their domain;
(2) *Student perceptions* (and indirectly, educators' perceptions) of motivational quality; and
(3) *Web site attributes* that will affect perceptions of motivational quality.

In the following sections, we describe the relationship between these factors and the balancing act that educators face when assessing Web resources.

Teacher Judgments of Content Validity

Content validity is priority No. 1! Before even considering other motivational concerns, the content must be *appropriate* for your teaching needs. It must support your instructional goals and learning objectives and satisfy the requirements of the activity or assignment. If one of the requirements is currency, the Web site should have an indicator of when it was last revised. If an obvious bias is present (or if the bias has not at least been identified by the authors), the site would likely be inappropriate. As an educator, you are the best judge of the appropriateness of the site for your needs. In Appendix A, we have included our *Content Validity Checklist*, a brief, handy reference for assessing content issues.

While the content may seem appropriate, it must also be verifiable, that is, valid. So, *authenticity* becomes important. The Web site must contain enough information about the authority source to allow the user to know the credibility of the source and be able to contact that source for clarification or additional information.

A number of instruments and a few Web sites deal very nicely with content issues. One notable one you may wish to explore is Kathy Schrock's Guide for Educators at http://www.capecod.net/kathyschrockguide/etc. This and other evaluation instruments are briefly discussed in Chapter Three.

When lesson-planning, it is the responsibility of the educator to decide whether a specific Web site measures up to his content validity criteria. An educator's judgment of appropriate and authentic content is a **necessary** but **insufficient** condition for a successful teaching episode. We think you know where this is going.

Students' Perceptions of Motivational Quality

Students' perceptions of the motivational quality of the Web site (and indirectly, the teacher or library media specialist's best guesstimate of students' potential perceptions of motivational quality) is a critical factor in a successful teaching episode using Web resources. That is, will the experience of interacting with the particular Web site you have chosen help motivate your students to learn? Will they want to stay in the Web site, look for links to related resources, and possibly re-visit the Web site for future learning opportunities after your lesson is over? Motivational quality can make or break a lesson. *Student perceptions* of motivational quality will ultimately determine the effectiveness of a Web site as a teaching/learning resource.

A Web resource with high motivational quality enhances the learning process. The degree of motivational quality is especially important if the student is doing independent research and has a choice between two or more Web sites to visit and use. It is also important for the educator who is selecting Web sites for use in teaching or for student assignments or activities.

And the Pivotal Factor: A Web Site's Motivational Attributes

A Web site's attributes or motivational dimensions will influence both student and teacher perceptions of motivational quality. In the context of E-V theory, a Web site that is stimulating and meaningful contributes to its value; one that is organized and easy-to-use promotes a positive expectation for success. The degree to which these qualities are present comprises the *motivational quality* of that Web site. Later in this chapter, we will explore these attributes further in the section entitled "Web Sites That Have What It Takes."

When judging a Web site's attributes and their effect on motivational quality, we certainly are not talking about its bells and whistles. The *value* (E-V Theory) issues include content criteria for judging the information contained within a Web site. These include accuracy, currency, clarity, validity, and comprehensive coverage of the topic. You are probably asking, "Aren't these the content validity criteria that were discussed under 'Teacher Judgments'?" Although they are content-related criteria, they can have an effect on student motivation, and therefore must also be included in a Web evaluation instrument that focuses on motivational quality. A Web site that contains accurate and unbiased information, which is provided by credible sources, increases the value of that site for the student. Conversely, a student may become frustrated at not finding enough or the right kind of information for his or her needs. In Part II, you will see that content issues are naturally addressed in the instrument and framed in terms of their effect on motivation.

You might also be wondering about functionality and whether that is a separate factor. Functionality is a popular topic when discussing Web sites. It includes technical issues and how well a site generally functions in terms of response time, links, navigation, and so on. Indeed, functionality is an important issue, especially since it affects motivation. When functionality is discussed in this book, then, it is framed in terms of its *effect on motivation*.

Putting It All Together

For successful teaching episodes, the educator must judge the content of the selected Web site to be appropriate and authentic. We assume that you, as the educator, are familiar with the specific content you have selected for a lesson and will make certain that whatever Web site you are considering using in your classroom or library media center has appropriate and authentic content. The motivational quality should be high. Motivational quality is based on students' perceptions of value and expectation for success. These perceptions are influenced by the Web site's attributes. Educators should also be able to project a Web site's potential motivational impact on students. We summarize the previous sections of this chapter by presenting a visual model that depicts the relationships among *teacher* judgments of content validity, *student* perceptions based on motivational quality, and the *attributes* in a Web site design that influence motivational quality. We call it the TSA Model for Web-Based Instruction.

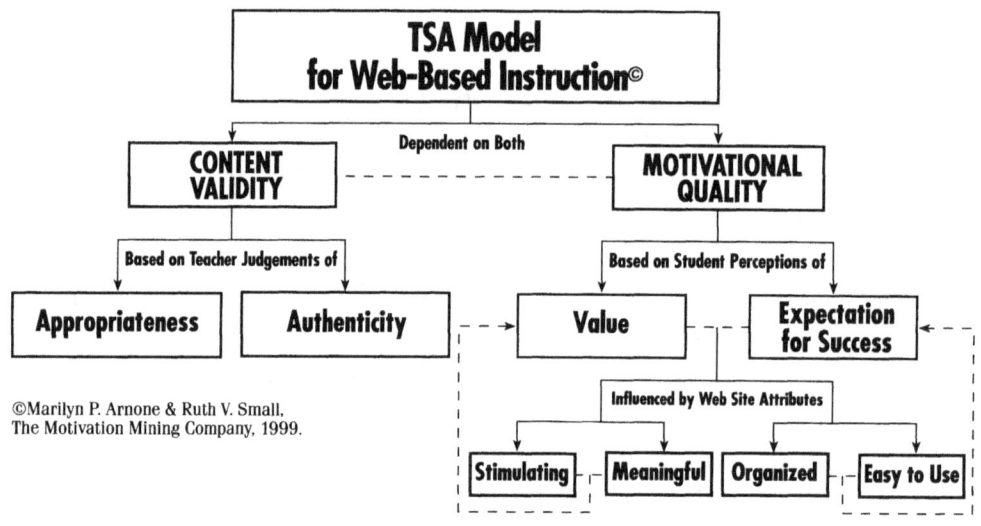

©Marilyn P. Arnone & Ruth V. Small,
The Motivation Mining Company, 1999.

Internet Gripes

You've probably had the experience of finding what you thought might be the perfect Web site for your lesson. The content was appropriate and thorough. There was no question about authority; the authors were identified and experts in their field. Then, disappointment set in. After interacting with the site as you prepared your lesson plan, you realized that other things about this site might actually undermine your instructional objectives. In this section, you'll find a few real gripes about Web sites that we've heard from educators who have participated in our seminars. They reviewed sites that might be applicable in a teaching situation. We will look at those gripes in light of what they say about the impact that such Web sites might have on motivation and learning. These are actual quotes.

Our first gripe came from an educator who reviewed a major broadcasting company's Web site, which she referred to as a "massive" site.

> *"A diverse range of interests is covered on this site... Getting lost or 'trapped' in some areas was easy. I did not always feel in control at this site, although it was an adventure. The links I chose to follow were active, although they never led outside of [Name of Web site]... The organization of headings and links seemed ad hoc at times. Buttons and maneuvering mechanisms were not consistent. In [one] section, they appeared primarily as text links at the bottom of the screen, but in [another] section they took a more graphical appearance at the top of the screen."*

What seems clear in the above quote is that this educator did not feel confident that she could successfully maneuver through this Web site. "I did not always feel in control at this site..." she said. She was further confused by its poor organization, and the *value* of the site seemed to be lessened by the fact that there were no links to sources outside the site itself. Do shortcomings like these have an effect on motivation? You bet. Remember earlier in this chapter when we defined motivation as the amount of effort one is willing to expend to achieve a desired outcome? Well, how long would you stay on task if you did not feel you had control of the situation? Most of us would move on to another site where we felt we might have a better chance of success in getting what we needed. This example illustrates nicely the *Expectation for Success* aspect of E-V theory.

If an adult had such difficulties with the Web site described above, imagine how elementary school-aged children would fare! Such a Web site would not be particularly useful in a lesson. Whether or not the site had appropriate content, if it was difficult to access or discover the navigational logic, then the experience of interacting with this site would be discouraging for anyone. We would *not expect to be successful.*

This next quote represents an educator who reviewed a genealogy Web site. She saw *value* in the information but was not successful at figuring out how to use it.

> *"The Web site was not clear and easy to read. When I searched for a surname it came up with a kind of shorthand of information and no clear pointers to where I could find the key to understand this. I know I value the kind of possible*

information I could get out of this Web site, but because it is confusing and not easy to read, I wonder if my skills are up to the challenge. I am after all only an amateur at genealogy."

Clearly, the Web site had information that she valued. So, it scored highly in that respect. Many sites may have lots of bells and whistles but lack the meat and potatoes. *Value*, or the personal relevance of the information, plays a big part in motivation. The question is, is it enough to overcome all the other shortcomings of a Web site? In this case, it is questionable. Did you notice a similar thread in her comments to the previous observations about an entirely different Web site? Again, there was an issue with confidence, that is, in the ability to successfully navigate within the Web site environment. Even worse, she began to question her own abilities. "...I wonder if my skills are up to the challenge...," she said.

Children will be even quicker to doubt their own competence in the face of such obstacles. As they learn critical evaluation skills, they will be better able to discern when problems are related to the Web site rather than internalize them as their own inadequacies.

What about sites that serve as jumping off points to lots of other great potential learning resources? This next educator found one that didn't stack up against the many really good ones. Her motivation went downhill as quickly as her tour.

"An all-in-one source of helpful Web sites is a great time-saver—if it works! However, my tour [of this Web site] plummeted downhill quickly as I attempted to connect with several links [unsuccessfully]."

The next educator reviewed a Web site on a city in the Northeast. She said that it contained a good deal of useful information that was well-organized and easy to follow. It was also easy to navigate. Sounds like it would be great site to introduce to upper elementary aged children. There was only one problem. It was boring. One sentence sums up her comments pretty succinctly.

"It is an excellent source of information but not very exciting to visit."

It is just not enough to have great information. Learners who label sites as "boring" do not usually hang in there long enough to get the information they need. We've talked about gripes for long enough. Now, let's talk about what makes a "pure grade" Web site!

Web Sites That Have What It Takes

"If motivation answers the 'why' of behavior, then the whys related to children's Web sites are: Why visit? Why stay? Why return? The answers to these questions lie in the motivational quality of the Web site."[14] Earlier in the chapter, we discussed some of the motivational attributes of Web sites that make them "valuable assets" (in motivation mining terms) to your lesson plans. Let's go into a bit more detail here about those attributes and provide a figure that illustrates their relationship to E-V theory.

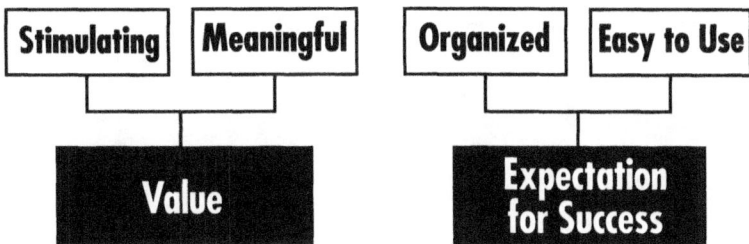

A *stimulating* Web site includes features that both capture and maintain interest and curiosity. Opportunities for interaction, exploration, and having fun also contribute to making a Web site stimulating. These features are especially important for engaging young learners. *Meaningful* refers to the usefulness, credibility and personal relevance of the Web site to the child. For example, the authenticity of the site's content and its appropriateness for the designated child audience would relate to personal relevance. Both these attributes contribute to the **Value** component of E-V theory.

The content of an *organized* Web site is well laid-out with a clear-cut structure, is free of typographical errors, and uses words that the designated audience can read and understand. Ease of navigation, user control, intact links, help mechanisms, and quick response speed are among the features of an *easy-to-use* Web site. These two attributes help to build the perception in the young users' mind that they can have a successful experience with the Web site. As mentioned earlier, the attributes can also help to boost students' confidence in their own abilities as information seekers. On the other hand, it is not uncommon that students question their own competence when they have poor experiences at a Web site. Both attributes relate to the **Expectation for Success** component of E-V theory.

We couldn't leave you with only "Internet Gripes" like the ones in the previous section. As *motivation miners*, we are always prospecting for positive Web experiences! One of our workshop participants found many of the qualities discussed above when she visited a Web site that we *can* name—the *Electronic Zoo*. She enjoyed the graphics and layout as well as the information.

Here is an excerpt from her comments:

> *"This site scored off the charts! It is an awesome site. I came away with the information I desired. I was motivated to remain in the site (could have stayed for hours), and definitely plan to return to this site."*

Her comments very nicely sum up this final point. A Web site that incorporates the motivational criteria we are talking about is likely to influence the child's tendency to remain in the site, revisit the Web site at another time, and to motivate others to visit the site as well.

COMING UP...

In Part II, Chapter Three, we discuss the *WebMAC Junior* motivational assessment tool and describe its development and testing.

ENDNOTES

[1] C. Kuhlthau, *Teaching the Library Research Process.* West Nyack, NY: The Center for Applied Research in Education Inc., 1985, p.7.

[2] V. H. Vroom, *Work and Motivation.* San Francisco: Jossey-Bass, 1995.

[3] F. G. Burton, Y. Chen, V. Grover, and K. A. Stewart, "An Application of Expectancy Theory for Assessing User Motivation to Utilize an Expert System. *Journal of Management Information Systems, 9* (3), Winter 1992-3, pp. 183-198.

[4] D. Hansen, "Lesson Evading and Lesson Dissembling: Ego Strategies in the Classroom". *American Journal of Education, 97,* 1989, pp.184-208.

[5] J. Brophy, *Motivating Students to Learn.* Boston: McGraw-Hill, 1998, p. 16.

[6] Brophy, 1998.

[7] R. J. Wlodkowski, *Enhancing Adult Motivation to Learn: A Guide to Improving Instruction and Increasing Learner Achievement.* San Francisco: Jossey-Bass Publishers, 1993, p. 8.

[8] Wlodkowski, 1993, p. 98.

[9] J.M. Keller, "Strategies for Stimulating the Motivation to Learn." *Performance & Instruction, 26* (8), October 1987, pp. 1-7.

[10] Burton et. al, 1992-3.

[11] K. C. Snead, Jr., and A. M. Harrell, "An Application of Expectancy Theory to Explain a Manager's Intention to Use a Decision Support System." *Decision Sciences, 25* (4), 1995, p.508.

[12] M. P. Arnone and R. V. Small, "Evaluating the Motivational Effectiveness of Children's Websites." *Educational Technology, 39* (2), March-April 1999.

[13] R. V. Small and M. P. Arnone, "Motivation Mining: Prospecting the Web." *The Book Report, 18* (1), May-June 1999, pp. 42-44.

[14] Arnone and Small 39 (2), 1999, p. 51.

HIGHLIGHTS
of Chapter Two

Motivation is often measured by how much effort one will expend on a task. It is an extremely important aspect of learning as not all the variation in the performance of individuals can be attributed to ability. Some of it can be attributed to one's motivation.

Motivation mining is a concept used to describe the identification and extraction of Web resources that have the potential to enhance student learning by meeting important motivational criteria. While content is a priority for educators when selecting Web sites for classroom or media center use, the site must also be motivating for the teaching episode to be a success. One without the other may lead to poor results in attaining the desired educational objectives.

Web sites created for children must be engaging and personally relevant. These elements contribute to one's perception of the value of a Web site. Web sites must also provide an environment that fosters an expectation for success.

Educators cite poor navigational and organizational aids as the aspects of some Web sites that decrease the motivation of users. These types of obstacles impact on one's confidence or belief that he can be successful in achieving his goals when visiting a Web site. They are particularly detrimental to children who may internalize their negative experience as incompetence on their parts. Web sites that are stimulating, meaningful, organized, and easy-to-use are likely to have learners coming back for more.

 **MINESTORMING**

Have you ever had an experience when you thought you had everything prepared and had selected just the right Web site for your class exercise, but things just didn't fly as you hoped they would? Is it possible that the Web site lacked motivational quality? What might you do differently next time? What could you suggest to improve the Web site's appeal, if anything? Jot down your ideas in the space below.

_____
_____
_____
_____
_____
_____
_____
_____
_____
_____

 **SELF-CHECK**

1) According to this taxonomy, evaluation is the highest form of learning. What taxonomy is it?

   _____

   _____

2) It is a simplified version of the *Big6* Model of Information Problem-Solving appropriate for very young learners. What is it called, and what does it emphasize?

   _____

   _____

3) Why is it important to evaluate Web-based resources?

   _____

   _____

4) What are some general categories of Web resources that educators might use?

   _____

   _____

5) What are three types of Web-based learning activities?

   _____

   _____

6) You can think of this as the amount of effort one is willing to expend on a task. What is it?

   _____

   _____

7) Why is it (i.e., your answer to Question #6) important?

   _____

   _____

8) What is the concept that refers to the examination of Web resources for their motivational potential or the potential to engage students in the learning process?

_____

_____

9) The TSA Model illustrates the relationship between which three factors?

_____

_____

10) How do things such as confusing organization and poor navigation contribute to a decrease in motivation?

_____

_____

SUGGESTED RESPONSES to Part I Self-Check

1) According to this taxonomy, evaluation is the highest form of learning. What taxonomy is it?

   Bloom's Taxonomy of Educational Objectives.

2) It is a simplified version of the *Big6* Model of Information Problem-Solving appropriate for very young learners. What is it called, and what does it emphasize?

   It is called the Super Three, and it emphasizes the flow of information from the Beginning, to the Middle, to the End.

3) Why is it important to evaluate Web-based resources?

   Since there is no requirement that Web sites be evaluated for issues that might concern the educator or user, it is up to them to evaluate on criteria they deem important.

4) What are some general categories of Web resources that educators might use?

   Educators may be interested in Ask-A services, federal and state government Web sites, commercial, and individual Web sites.

5) What are three types of Web-based learning activities?

   Communications, information retrieval, and information sharing.

6) You can think of this as the amount of effort one is willing to expend on a task. What is it?

   Motivation.

7) Why is it (i.e., your answer to Question #6) important?

   Motivation accounts for much of the variation in achievement, which cannot be attributed to ability alone. Motivation is a critical component of lifelong learning and of self-directed learners.

8) What is the concept that refers to the examination of Web resources for their motivational potential or the potential to engage students in the learning process?

   Motivation mining.

9) The TSA Model illustrates the relationship between which three factors?

   It describes the relationship between teacher judgments of content validity, students' perceptions of motivational quality, and a Web site's motivational attributes.

10) How do things such as confusing organization and poor navigation contribute to a decrease in motivation?

    They tend to decrease one's confidence in his or her ability to have a successful experience at the Web site. Sometimes, it can even result in a perception of oneself as incompetent when, in fact, the site is at fault.

Part II

Mining Tools for a Motivational Assessment

CHAPTER 3

Using a Motivational Assessment Tool to Evaluate Web Resources

Introduction

Although there are a number of Web evaluation tools available, few are designed for children to use as tools that can teach them a structured method for evaluating Web sites.[1] Virtually none focus on the motivational aspects of Web sites, such as those features that motivate students to visit, stay and explore, and return to a Web site. In Chapter Three, we describe some existing Web site evaluation instruments, explain the development and testing of the *WebMAC* instruments focusing primarily on *WebMAC Junior–2000*, and finally offer three ways Web site motivational assessment tools can be used.

Chapter Objectives

By the end of this chapter, you will:
- be familiar with several Web site evaluation instruments.
- understand the differences between the *WebMAC* instruments and other web evaluation instruments.
- be able to describe three ways of using Web-based motivational assessment tools.
- be familiar with the development and testing of the *WebMAC* instruments.

Existing Web Evaluation Instruments

Educator and evaluation specialist Kathleen Schrock emphasizes the importance of educators' feeling comfortable with the resources they select to incorporate into their teaching. "Teachers should be able to evaluate sites critically, examine the technical aspects of the site, the authority of the writer, and the validity of the writer's content."[2] She conducted a brief review of a number of articles and general evaluation instruments. Her report can be found in the *ERIC Digest*. *ERIC Digests* are free and are available online at this URL: http://ericir.syr.edu.

Because of their dynamic, interactive nature, Web sites require different criteria for evaluation than some of the other more traditional types of media (e.g., print, video). A number of excellent evaluation instruments help educators judge the suitability of a Web site for instructional needs. Some focus heavily on content and validity issues (Does it have the right information?), while others focus on functionality issues (Does it work the way it is supposed to?).

Most of these instruments, with the exception of Kathy Schrock's, were designed for use by librarians and teachers to assess the appropriateness of Web sites. Few were created for independent use by students or as a tool for teaching students a structured method for evaluating Web sites. Although useful, few are theoretically based and offer diagnostic methods for assessing and interpreting results. We introduce some other well-known Web evaluation instruments below and encourage readers to visit any or all of these sites to review them in more depth.

Carolyn Caywood's *Library Selection Criteria for WWW Resources* instrument specifies evaluation criteria in three categories (access, design, content). Each category contains a comprehensive list of related questions. There is no scoring mechanism, analysis, or interpretation process described. The instrument is intended for use by librarians in assessing a Web site's value to its users.
<http://www6.pilot.infi.net/~carolyn/criteria.html>

Esther Grassian's *Thinking Critically About World Wide Web Resources* instrument has four categories of "points to consider" (Content & Evaluation, Source & Date, Structure, and Other). There is no scoring mechanism, and no analysis/interpretation method is included. The author provides helpful links to additional resources including *Guiding Children Through Cyberspace—URLs*, a page that lists Web sites for guiding children's home use of the Internet (e.g., software reviews, ratings of Web sites).
<http://www.library.ucla.edu/libraries/college/instruct/>

Karen McLachlan developed a set of three web evaluation instruments called *Cyberguides*. Two instruments rate content, and a third evaluates Web site design. Each instrument consists of eight general areas of assessment (e.g., speed, content/information) with several criteria for each area (e.g., "The home page downloads efficiently enough to use during whole class instruction," "The information is clearly labeled and organized, and will be easily understood by my students," and so on). Her instruments use a numerical rating system and include an interpretation of one's total score. It does not break that score down by category or item nor does it provide visual representation of scores.
<http://www.cyberbee.com/guides.html>

Kathy Schrock has developed three versions of her *Critical Evaluation Survey* for students at different levels (elementary, middle, and secondary). Each instrument begins by asking the student some questions about how they accessed the site and what site they are evaluating. The elementary school version contains 18 main questions, the middle school version has 24 main questions, and the secondary school version has 35 main questions. Most questions are answered with a simple "yes" or "no." All versions ask for qualitative summary responses. No scoring mechanism or

analysis/interpretation method is included.
<http://discoveryschool.com/schrockguide/evalmidd.html>

All of these instruments are useful for evaluating Web sites. Recently, however, we developed a unique set of evaluation instruments that focus on motivational quality while encompassing content and functionality issues from a motivational perspective. Each of these instruments has a detailed scoring and interpretation process. Furthermore, these instruments were created primarily for children to use independently or for educators to use as an instructional tool to help students learn to evaluate Web sites.

The Web Site Motivational Analysis Checklist

The *Web Site Motivational Analysis Checklist* (known as *WebMAC*, for short) is a series of Web evaluation instruments designed for evaluators from grade 1 to adult. They are based on Expectancy-Value Theory applied to the Web environment, as discussed in the previous chapter. The series includes instruments specifically created for use in educational, business, or entertainment contexts. These instruments have been tested and validated, resulting in several major modifications and revisions from the original instrument.[3] The *WebMAC* instruments are intended to identify areas for improvement of an existing Web site and provide guidance for the design of a new Web site. They are widely used as materials in teaching children to evaluate Web resources.

A set of eight instruments was developed. These instruments distinguish themselves from existing web evaluation instruments because they:
▶ are student-centered.
▶ are theoretically based.
▶ focus on motivational issues.
▶ have been tested and validated.
▶ incorporate a variety of methods for analysis and interpretive feedback.

Each of the instruments contains items on important aspects of evaluation such as content credibility, currency, navigation, links, and organization. In some way, each of these aspects has a major impact on motivation, which accounts for student behaviors such as persistence on a task (e.g., amount of time a student will continue to explore for information at a given site). It also affects whether or not a student will return to a site to learn more at another time. Let's consider the content validity aspect of evaluating Web sites. A Likert-type agreement scale, such as *WebMAC Middle*, includes this item related to content validity: "The information at this Web site is accurate and unbiased." From a motivation perspective, it relates to the

Value dimension. Discovering you had inaccurate content for a school project would be frustrating and discouraging. A return visit to that site would be unlikely. In *WebMAC Junior–2000*, that same *Value* item (in question format) is greatly simplified and reads: "Was the information at this Web site believable? (Did it seem to be true?)." An item like this can be a catalyst for discussion. The teacher or LMS can encourage students to think about clues on a Web site that would help answer the question, such as information on the author or organization that put up the site.

Items like "Was it easy to find your way around without getting lost?" refer to the navigational aspects of Web sites. In terms of motivation, how easy or difficult it is to navigate affects a child's confidence and expectation that he or she can be successful in a particular Web site environment. So, in using the *WebMAC* instruments, you will see many questions that relate to the critical evaluation issues that we are all concerned about; the *WebMAC* instruments, however, take such concerns to another level by framing them in motivational terms. This serves a twofold purpose in education: It makes the instruments valuable to both (1) students who are learning evaluation skills and (2) educators who use the instruments as lesson-planning and design tools and must consider the all-important contribution of motivation to learning.

WebMAC Junior—2000

The *Web Site Motivational Analysis Checklist (WebMAC) Junior–2000* is a Web evaluation tool for students in grades one through four, but has also been used in grades five and six, as well. It was designed to help our youngest students diagnose, analyze, and assess Web sites *from a child's perspective* — critical skills for the new millennium in which today's young students become tomorrow's leaders.

WebMAC Junior–2000 (*WebMAC Junior*, for short) lets students rate the motivational quality of various aspects of a Web site and plot the scores on a grid, allowing quick visual assessment of the strengths and weaknesses of that site. The instrument may be used by an individual student or with an entire class. The reasonable length of the instrument permits students to easily pinpoint specific areas in need of improvement. The instrument may also be used by teachers for selecting Web sites to use in their lessons or as guidelines for developing new Web sites or improving existing ones. In Chapter Eight, we offer some ideas for using this instrument in the context of integrating information literacy instruction with the curriculum, while in Chapter Nine we offer other uses for the instrument.

In the next few chapters, you will become familiar with *WebMAC*

Junior–2000's administration guidelines. We'll discuss providing students with definitions of several common Web site terms (e.g., home page, button, link), step-by-step directions for completing and scoring the instrument, how to help students interpret their results, and ideas for curriculum-related activities.

The *WebMAC Junior–2000* contains 16 items (eight *Value*; eight *Expectation for Success*) in question form and uses smiley faces for recording responses. It also includes two YES/NO questions and two places to write qualitative responses (i.e., what the young evaluator liked best about the site and what might be done to improve the site). Examples of items for the *Value* and *Expectation for Success* categories are:

> VALUE: *Was the information you found at this Web site useful to you?*
>
> EXPECTATION FOR SUCCESS: *Did all the parts of this Web site work the way they should?*

WebMAC Junior–2000 was preceded by a longer version of the instrument which is now called *WebMAC Junior Long Form*. The *Long Form* is included in Appendix D. It contains 24 items (12 Value; 12 Expectation for Success) in question form and also uses smiley faces for recording responses, as well as YES/NO and open-ended questions. Examples of the *Long Form*'s additional *Value* and *Expectation for Success* items are:

> VALUE: *Did you learn new things by visiting this Web site?*
>
> EXPECTATION FOR SUCCESS: *Were the pictures, cartoons, and other visuals clear and easy to see?*

WebMAC Junior–2000 is included in Chapter Five. In Chapters Six and Seven, we explain scoring the instrument for the two dimensions and interpreting the results.

We also include *Web Site Investigator* in Appendix E.[4] Adapted from the *WebMAC Junior* instruments, it is a very brief questionnaire that consists of only 12 items and no scoring grids. It may be useful for very young children or when only a simple introduction to evaluation of Web sites is warranted.

WebMAC Middle

WebMAC Middle targets students in grades 5-8. It contains 24 statements (12 *Value*; 12 *Expectation for Success*). Rather than using smiley faces and a question format, *WebMAC Middle* uses declarative statements and a scale based on degree of agreement. Examples of *WebMAC Middle* statements for each category are:

VALUE: "I find the information at this Web site to be current and up-to-date."

EXPECTATION FOR SUCCESS: "All the Web site's links work the way they should."

Middle school educators or upper elementary educators who desire a more sophisticated instrument for their students can find the complete *WebMAC Middle* instrument plus scoring instructions, tally sheet, and plotting grids in Appendix C.

Other *WebMAC* Instruments

WebMAC Junior—2000, WebMAC Junior Long Form, Web Site Investigator, and *WebMAC Middle* are four of the eight *WebMAC* instruments (all four are contained in this book). We will briefly introduce some other WebMAC evaluation instruments below, pointing out how they differ from the instruments presented in this book.

▶ *WebMAC Senior*: Designed for use by students in grades 9 and up. It is featured in our companion book *WWW Motivation Mining: Finding Treasures for Teaching Evaluation Skills (Grades 9-12)*. That book also includes *WebMAC Middle* and a number of ideas from high school and middle school teachers and library media specialists on how to these instruments with older students. It also includes ways college professors are using the instrument to refine their course Web sites.

▶ *WebMAC Broadcast/Cable*: Intended for children's television producers to use to assess their program-related Web sites. The instrument has 28 items (plus open-ended questions) and contains many of the same questions as *WebMAC Junior Long Form* as well as additional ones that pertain specifically to television programs.

▶ *WebMAC Professional*: Designed for use by educators, Web designers, instructional designers, and others when participating in an online Web site review panel. Its purpose is to assess the motivational effectiveness of Web sites targeted toward educators.

▶ *WebMAC Business*: Intended for businesses to assess their commercial Web sites. It is currently in its final stages of testing and revision.

Development and Testing

The *WebMAC* instruments have been continuously tested since they were first developed in 1997. More than 70 preservice and inservice classroom teachers and library professionals participated in their original pilot testing. Pilot testing with professionals allowed us to identify vague or inconsistent language, redundant items, length of time to complete, and level of ease of directions for administering and scoring. Following each test, the instrument was revised and refined.

Even in the earliest stages of evaluating the *WebMAC* instruments, pilot testers had overwhelmingly positive comments about them. Some of their comments appear below:

"...very informative and a good tool."

"...questions were very easy to answer."

"...simple to use self-scoring and easy to interpret."

"...an excellent tool to use to really evaluate a site for its true value."

"...this instrument was very well designed and functional... easy to understand and use."

"...filling it out was a satisfying experience in itself; I enjoyed reflecting about my experience at the site."

" I also see [the instrument] as an excellent tool to use to help students learn for themselves how to judge the quality of different Web sites."

All the feedback from educators was critical to the development of the instruments, but we still needed to hear from the children themselves.

From the Original *WebMAC Junior* to the Present

The original *WebMAC Junior* was put to the test in classrooms and library media centers across the country throughout 1998 and early-1999. The feedback was extremely helpful because educators could now tell us how the actual users were responding. Thus, in about a year's time, we progressed through several versions as we continued to fine-tune the instrument.

In early-1999, *WebMAC Junior* was still 24 items plus the qualitative section. Then, several LMSs mentioned that a shorter instrument would actually be more helpful to them. With that, we asked some of the former users of the instrument if they also felt a shorter instrument would be beneficial. Overwhelmingly, the answer was "Yes." A shorter instrument would help in terms of the limited time available to administer the instrument, the attention spans of the younger children, and the cost of copying. We decided that the longer 24-item questionnaire, now called *WebMAC Junior Long Form*, would still be an excellent resource for Web site designers and for those with fewer restrictions on time and budget. However, we now were inspired to develop a new version of the instrument, and that, of course, meant more testing!

A Pilot Study in Pennsylvania

One of the strongest proponents for a new shorter version of *WebMAC Junior* was Melissa Yates, Library Coordinator for the Central Bucks County (Pennsylvania) Elementary Schools and LMS at Buckingham (Pennsylvania) Elementary School. She even offered to pilot the new instrument with a large number of students and involve interested LMSs from other schools in the area. This was an offer we couldn't refuse and we got right to work on the creation of what we now call *WebMAC Junior–2000*! So, if you like the new instrument, thank Melissa and her colleagues for putting it to the test!

First, we carefully screened every question on the 24-item questionnaire and kept what we felt were the most critical items. Melissa and several others helped us hone it down. We also needed to make sure that the items were equally distributed between *Value* items and *Expectation for Success* items. Some of the items that were dropped related more to the aesthetic appeal of Web sites. We kept the two qualitative questions at the end. We were able to reduce the instrument enough so that it could be photocopied on two sheets of paper. Then, we had to modify the scoring templates and plotting grids to reflect the reduced number of items. When one of the authors handed the new instrument and administration directions over to Melissa in her LMC (Library Media Center), she breathed a sigh of relief combined with just the slightest bit of trepidation, hoping that the new instrument would work at least as well as the former.

Altogether, more than 500 students used the new instrument in Bucks County, Pennsylvania! The library media specialists returned the filled-in instruments of their students (without children's names, of course) to us. They were separated according to grade level (grades 2, 3, and 4). Several schools reviewed the same Web sites so that we could later do an analysis of student responses, item by item. The feedback we received from each LMS who participated in the study has further helped us to refine the instrument that you will find in Chapter Five of this book. We are grateful to all of them and to their students for helping us to accomplish this goal. What follows are some highlights of the useful feedback they gave us.

The response to the new instrument was excellent. According to Melissa who used it with about 80 second and third graders at Buckingham Elementary School, the shorter instrument was "very doable in the time span that I have the children." She also said that the instrument was right for their attention span; the children could understand all the questions and were motivated to do it. We should mention that Melissa read aloud each question, which has proven to be an excellent way to use the "Junior" instruments with children in grades 1-3.

Kathy Sweeney, LMS at Titus Elementary School, Warminster, Pennsylvania, also supports reading the questions aloud before giving the questionnaire to students. She pilot tested the instrument with 75 third and fourth graders. She did not read the questions aloud to either group. In retrospect, she feels that some of her less-experienced (with the Internet) third graders would have benefited from having the questions read aloud before working on it themselves. The older students, on the other hand, were fine on their own. "The fourth graders," Kathy said, "were much more capable of 'the job' and attacked it quickly. They were able to understand the smiley faces, what they meant, read the questions, and decide which face matched what they thought should be the answer. They had a much easier time."

LMS Jennifer Skilton was responsible for piloting the instrument with about 300 students at Barclay and Warwick Elementary Schools in Central Bucks County. She is fortunate enough to have a mini-lab with 15 computers and another nine or 10 computers spread throughout her library. She chose Web sites that tied in with what students were learning in class. "I try to connect everything to what they are doing in the classroom. I don't believe in teaching in a vacuum, especially in the library," she said. After preparing the students for the evaluation exercise, including reviewing all the questions and discussing what they meant, Jennifer allowed the students to peruse the sites on their own, filling in the instrument as they went along.

Jennifer feels that using the instrument helps give students a focus when evaluating Web sites. "I think they enjoyed it, too, because it did give them a focus [while looking at the site] rather than saying, 'OK, here is the Internet. Here is the Web site. Find your way through it.'"

She said that students really paid attention to the questions on the instrument. For example, on one of the Web sites related to pyramids, there appeared to be a technical problem. "There is one part," Jennifer explained, "where supposedly you can go into the Sphinx, and it wasn't working. So, [students] found the question that says 'Is the Web site working the way it should?' They said, 'We can't give it a happy face for that!' So they are really connecting."

Plotting their scores on a grid was new to many students. "Some of the third graders got it right away, and others didn't. It really depends on where they are in math," explained Jennifer. She used an overhead transparency to demonstrate how to plot the scores. When students eventually got it, she said you could see that it "clicked." We were interested in how the younger grades would do, but we suggest that plotting scores will generally work best with students in the upper elementary grades.

Nearly 50 second graders used *WebMAC Junior* at Gayman Elementary School, in Danboro, Pennsylvania. LMS Susan Angstadt-Sullivan told us that her students were proud to help in pilot testing the new instrument. "When I told them about it, you could see them sit up in their chairs with their chests puffed out a little," she said. Susan used a clever idea to get her students into the swing of rating items using the questionnaire's smiley faces; she had them make their own faces and describe what their faces meant. Using faces as a rating system worked well for this age group, according to Susan. They understood the meaning and the idea of rating in this way. "It was very effective," she said.

Most students were able to fill in the open-ended questions at the end of the instrument, but a few did not fill in that section due to "writing ability," Susan told us. Students at this age will vary greatly in that respect.

Her students evaluated an art-related Web site. For that reason, it was not the kind of site that they would associate with doing research for a school project. Two questions, however, specifically referred to "information," which confused children because of the context in which they were using the instrument. One question read "Was it easy to find the information you needed?" Since they were reviewing an art site, it didn't fit as well in this situation. "The children are very literal. Students looking for graphics wouldn't associate 'information' with graphics," she said. By changing that question to "Was it easy to find what you needed on this Web site?" it made it applicable to all situations, including finding written information, graphics, sound bites, and even entertainment. The other confusing question read "How useful was this Web site for getting the information you needed?" Again, we made the question more generic by rewriting it as "Was what you found on this Web site useful to you?" This improved the use of the instrument for younger students, and it still works well for older elementary students. For example, when a fourth grade student, uses a particular Web site to collect *information* for a research project, the student naturally associates the first question (How easy was it to find what you needed on this Web site?) with whether or not he easily found the *information* he needed.

Susan commented that pilot testing the instrument was lots of fun for both her students and herself. She even plans on using the instrument with other grade levels as well.

Jill Talarico also agreed that changing the wording of the two items that used the word "information" would be an improvement, although it did not pose a specific problem in her situation. She is the LMS at Kutz Elementary School in Doylestown, Pennsylvania. She used the instrument with about 50 third graders students who reviewed the same site on Pyramids that Jennifer Skilton's students evaluated. Like Jennifer's students, Jill's students were disappointed in the functionality aspects of the Web site, which they discussed when they got back into groups after rating the site in pairs. "A lot of them came up with the conclusion that it wasn't the easiest site, or that it took too long for things to download, and that it wasn't very user-friendly," Jill said. "They were pretty honest about it. They were into being the evaluators. They were really discussing 'What do you think?' They were talking about it and not just circling faces," she observed.

Again, we found that the rating scale worked well with these third graders and scoring was not a problem. "They liked the happy faces... I think they really enjoyed using it... I think it made it easier for them. They didn't have to think about numbers and averages. They could just pick a face," Jill said. She did not use the scoring grid with these students as time was limited to just one class period.

Jill had seen the *WebMAC Junior Long Form* at a librarian meeting held at Kutz Elementary where local LMSs discussed evaluating Web sites. "I definitely like the shorter form," Jill said. She felt the shorter form encouraged students to be more thoughtful about their responses because they didn't lose interest quickly. "I remember thinking the longer form would be a little too much for them to handle. They would have lost attention and circled anything instead of really thinking about it."

The pilot study in Pennsylvania was a tremendous help in fine-tuning the instrument you will find in Chapter Five, *WebMAC Junior–2000*. Hats off to all the LMSs and students who participated! As you can see, the "Junior" instrument has undergone quite a metamorphosis since its beginnings. That is what development and testing is all about. We hope that you will benefit from this preliminary work by having a successful experience using it with your students.

Three Ways to Use Web Site Motivational Assessment

There are a number of ways you can use the Web site motivational assessment tools provided in this book. As we present each of these ways, we will provide a scenario that illustrates its implementation.

1. A Teaching Tool.

You can use *WebMAC Junior–2000* or one of the other *WebMAC* instruments as a teaching tool to help your students learn valuable evaluation skills. In this way, your students will understand how important evaluation can be when it comes to electronic resources on the Web, and you can feel assured that they are using high-quality resources.

SCENARIO #1

Alexis Plavocos, the library media specialist at Jefferson Elementary School is teaching the Big6 to all of the third grade classes in the school. In order to make the lessons more meaningful to the students, Alexis meets with each of the grade level teams throughout the year to determine what areas of the curriculum they will emphasize and what assignments and other learning activities the students will be working on.

Alexis knows that the third graders are currently completing small group projects on their favorite authors. The students are required to develop an oral presentation for a school assembly using both print and electronic resources. Although students understand that the resources they use in the library have undergone a rigid selection process, they need to know that the resources they find on the Internet have had no such scrutiny.

So Alexis teaches the students about the importance of evaluation and introduces them to *WebMAC Junior—2000*. She shows them an example of a Web site that she has evaluated using the instrument and has them practice in their small groups with a given site. Then Alexis collects the scores for each group, plots the scores on the scoring grid, and posts all of the grids on the library's bulletin board so students can review and compare scores.

As the students work on their group projects, they use *WebMAC Junior—2000* to evaluate the Web sites they encounter in their research. Alexis overhears some spirited debates about some sites. By using this questionnaire to assess the motivational quality of Web sites, the students had more confidence about which sites to incorporate into their presentations.

2. A Lesson Planning Tool.

Using the Web in classroom presentations or as part of student activities and assignments has become commonplace. You already may be a highly motivating teacher, but to make learning happen, you also must be certain that the Web resources you select are also highly motivating. So, how do you know if the Web sites you have chosen are high-quality sites? You don't, unless you evaluate them. You may find *WebMAC Middle* useful as a *lesson-planning tool* to help you make important decisions about whether a particular site may or may not be appropriate for your teaching objectives not only from a content validity perspective but also from a motivational perspective. Here's another scenario to illustrate the use of the instrument.

SCENARIO #2

The team of fifth grade language arts teachers are planning a unit on censorship to kick off a project in which students will have to conduct research in order to debate the issues related to the topic. They want to start with a dynamic lesson and are looking for materials to help them plan and implement the lesson.

When one of the teachers types the keyword into a search engine, he receives dozens of potential Web sites with text, audio, and video information that he wants to incorporate into his lesson. The teachers know they can't use them all, so they divide up the sites, and each teacher uses *WebMAC Middle* to help identify the most credible and motivating information on the Web and decide which sites to integrate into their unit. The team is able to narrow the search down to three "Awesome" Web sites.

---

3. A RESEARCH AND DEVELOPMENT TOOL.

You may also find *WebMAC Junior–2000* valuable as a *research and development tool*. You can use it (by answering the questions from the perspective of your students) to conduct your own research comparing the motivational effectiveness of various sites containing the same type of content. Or, you may be interested in researching the effect of motivational quality of Web sites on learning outcomes. You or your students may also use the tool's items as guidelines for developing your own class or school Web site. Here is our final scenario that illustrates the use of *WebMAC Junior–2000* for research and development.

SCENARIO #3

Sean Johnstone, a sixth grade teacher, is working with his class to design a class Web site. Sean asks each of the students to identify one or two exemplary existing class Web sites by using *WebMAC Junior—2000* to rate the sites they find. Sean then meets with the students to discuss the design of their Web site, which incorporates some of their favorite features from the exemplary sites with their own original ideas.

After the students complete the initial development of their class Web site, Sean arranges with the sixth grade teachers at another middle school in the district to evaluate the class Web site and share the results with his students. The teachers teach their students to use *WebMAC Junior—2000* and require them to use the instrument to assess the fledgling site. Each class tallies and plots their scores on the *WebMAC* grid. Sean's class uses the results to improve and enhance their site before finally posting it to the Web and announcing the site to the rest of the school.

COMING UP...

In the next three chapters, you'll find everything you'll need to use *WebMAC Junior–2000* with your students. We begin with complete administration directions in Chapter Four.

ENDNOTES

[1] R.V. Small and M. P. Arnone, "Evaluating Web Resources with Young Children." *Library Talk, 12* (3), May-June 1999, pp. 14-16.

[2] K. Schrock. "Evaluation of World Wide Web Sites: An Annotated Bibliography." *ERIC Digest*, June 1998. (EDO-IR-98-02)

[3] R. V. Small, "Assessing the Motivational Quality of World Wide Web Sites." *ERIC Digest*, 1997. (ED407930)

[4] M. P. Arnone and R. V. Small, "Web Site Investigator." *Crinkles, 1* (6), July-August 1999, p. 37.

HIGHLIGHTS of Chapter Three

Chapter Three outlined several existing evaluation instruments that have been helpful to educators and LMSs. The *WebMAC* instruments were then introduced focusing particularly on the development and testing leading to the new *WebMAC Junior–2000*. A pilot study of more than 500 students in Bucks County, Pennsylvania, led to the newest version of the instrument. Educators from across the country have found the *WebMAC* instruments to be useful tools for teaching children critical evaluation skills. The *WebMAC* instruments can be used as (1) a teaching tool, (2) a lesson-planning tool, and (3) a research and development tool.

 **MINESTORMING**

Use the space below to record some of the great thoughts and ideas you've generated from reading Chapter Three.

_____
_____
_____
_____
_____
_____
_____
_____
_____

Chapter 4

Administering the Instrument

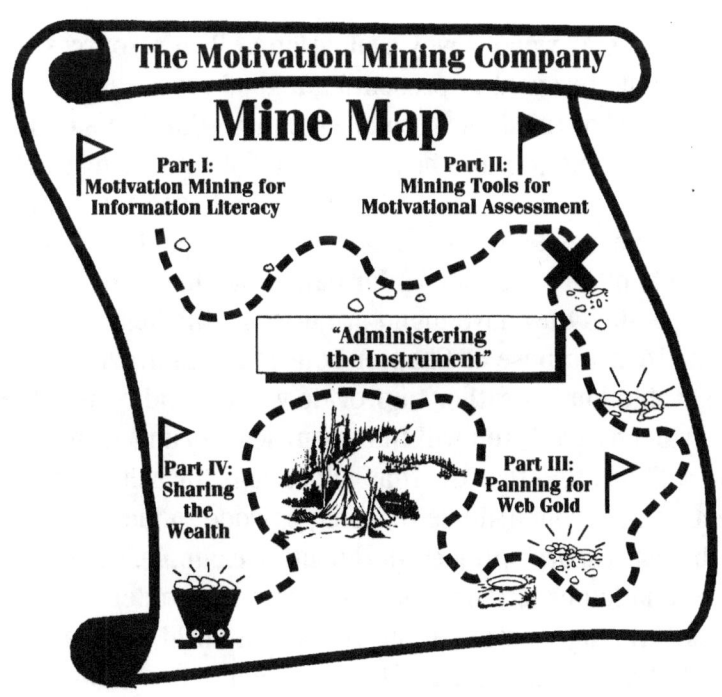

Introduction

The *Web Site Motivational Analysis Checklist (WebMAC) Junior–2000* for elementary school students is intended to assess the motivational quality of a Web Site-its appeal, usefulness, and ease of use. As described in the previous chapter, it may be used by an individual, small group, or with an entire class. In this chapter, you will find complete directions for administering *WebMAC Junior–2000* to your students or for using it yourself. In our discussions with practitioners, we have found a wide range of time allocations; that is, anywhere from a single class session to teaching the use of the instrument in conjunction with a larger unit on evaluation that spans several sessions.

Chapter Objectives

By the end of Chapter Four, you will:
▶ be familiar with ways to prepare students prior to using *WebMAC Junior–2000*
▶ be able to administer the instrument to students.

Setting the Stage

Students may wonder why evaluation of Web resources is necessary. Some time should be spent in presenting a good case. As many of our colleagues have confirmed, most children believe that if it's on the Internet, it must be good information. You heard one way of convincing students otherwise in Chapter One when LMS Gail Gilland used the Columbine Massacre as an example. You will hear another from Linda Zuber in Chapter Eight. Students often experience information overload, not knowing which of the many Web Sites they have found are actually the best ones to use for their assignments.[1] The purpose of Chapter Four is not to provide you with a lesson or unit on evaluation but rather to provide you with administrative guidelines for the instrument itself. You will find many lesson/unit ideas in Chapter Eight. You will also find that the time allocations for using the *WebMAC* instruments range from a single teaching episode to incorporating it as part of a month-long research project. In the latter example, the effects of the *WebMAC* evaluation experience remained with the students as they applied the same criteria to a new situation with a real-world application.

While Internet use is occurring more and more at home, you should not presuppose that younger students will understand all its conventions by any means. Before having students review a Web site, make sure they understand some common terms used in discussing Web sites. For example, a *home page* is the starting place. Here you find out what is on the Web Site. A link is a way of connecting to another source of information. A *button* is what you click in order to move from one place to another within the Web site or to activate a particular request. They can be of any shape or size but it should be clear by their label or image what each one is meant to do. You could give them the example of a picture of a house commonly used as a button (or icon) to bring the user back to the *home page*.

Defining common terms may not seem to be necessary if the students already have experience with the World Wide Web, but those who do not may feel embarrassed to admit their inexperience. Sometimes, it is helpful to simply call it a "review."

Providing an Overview of the Web Site

Most likely, you will have preselected one or more sites for your students to review. Once students are comfortable with Web site conventions and terminology, you can provide them with an overview of the specific site that they will evaluate using the following suggestions:

▶ Discuss the general topic or subject matter of the Web site. For example, if the Web site is science-related, briefly tell the children what to expect.
▶ Take just a few minutes to explore the Web site with your students to give them some preliminary familiarity with its basic content and structure before they really take the time to explore. Either you can give them a couple of minutes to do this on their own or with a small group, or you can demonstrate yourself.

Some Web sites have links to other sites or have affiliated subsites that contain as much or more information on the desired topic. The primary site (e.g., used the most to accomplish the targeted goal) is the one that should be evaluated with your students. If the main site and links, or subsites, are heavily used, each should be evaluated separately.

Interacting with the Web Site

There are two basic approaches that we found educators like to take with this. Some prefer to give students about 15 minutes or more to explore and interact with the Web site. Students either do this individually or within a small group. After giving students this free exploration time, they provide each child or small group with the *WebMAC* instrument. They then read the directions for the instrument and allow students time to complete the questions.

The second approach is to hand out the instrument first. Then, the teacher or LMS reads the directions for the instrument. The students are allowed to explore and interact with the Web site and fill out the questionnaire as they wish. When using this approach, the students will need more time since they are exploring and using the questionnaire at the same time. This approach works best for older students who do not require that each question be read aloud.

Giving Students Directions

If you wish to take a peek at *WebMAC Junior–2000* in Chapter Five now, feel free to do so. It may help to get familiar with some of the items before reading on. Students should understand that they will be evaluating the quality of the Web site. Quality can be explained in terms of how interesting or useful the site is and how well it works. Use Overhead Transparencies #2 and #3 in Chapter Twelve to help explain quality.

Read the directions aloud including the example item so that each child understands clearly that *WebMAC Junior–2000* is not a test but rather a way for them to hone their skills as young evaluators. The "Instructions" included with the instrument suggest that students consider themselves judges like those in an art or science fair. Make sure to emphasize that THERE ARE NO RIGHT OR WRONG ANSWERS! It seems that the youngest children have a difficult time with this because they are so eager to please their teacher or LMS, and they think that giving positive responses will do so.

If you are working with very young children or children with low reading abilities, it may be necessary to read each question aloud. Having the class use their rulers to help keep their place also may help. You could then say, "Put your ruler under the faces for question number one. Listen carefully. (*Read question.*) Think about your experience with this Web site. Then, circle the face that shows how you feel." Repeat the instructions, if necessary. This may seem restrictive when, ideally, the students could fill out the questionnaire as they are exploring their Web site; but for some groups, this is the best approach. Alternatively, you should at least spend some time reading the questions aloud as a preparation for children to fill in answers on their own.

It will not be necessary to be quite as explicit with older students who can generally use the instrument on their own.

In Chapter Twelve, you will find a number of overhead transparency masters which you could use when introducing *WebMAC Junior–2000*.

You As the Model

There is one other thing we almost forgot to mention about working with and administering *WebMAC Junior–2000*. That's you! If you model enthusiasm for information exploration and evaluation of information resources, you can help to spark a similar enthusiasm in your students. After all, if competence and information literacy is the *destination* we hope our students will reach, then we should help to make their *journey* exciting and fun! Modeling enthusiasm and showing empathy for our learners can help in achieving that goal.

Ours Is Not the Only Way

We have simply offered you some suggestions for administering the instrument. We have not provided an actual lesson plan. There have been so many creative ways that educators have used this and the other *WebMAC* instruments that the administration procedures have varied from one instance to another. It's really up to you. Some educators have told us that they feel the instrument is best used as part of a larger unit that integrates information literacy and the curriculum. We agree. To make the most of this evaluation tool, it should be used after students have been exposed to evaluation as an information literacy skill. How and in what context it is used will have an impact on how you administer the instrument. You'll find a number of innovative lesson ideas in Chapter Eight that were shared with us by teachers and LMSs from around the country.

COMING UP...

WebMAC Junior–2000 is on its way!

ENDNOTES

[1] R. V. Small and M. P. Arnone, "Web Site Quality: Do Students Know It When They See It?" *School Library Media Activities Monthly,* XV (6), February 1999.

HIGHLIGHTS of Chapter Four

In Chapter Four, a number of suggestions on administering *WebMAC Junior–2000* including two approaches that have been used were offered. It was also suggested that the different ways educators have been using this tool might indicate alternative administration procedures based on the context in which it is used. Creative liberty is encouraged. Lastly, we suggested that you, as an educator, have a great deal of motivational influence on your learners when it comes to modeling enthusiasm for information exploration and evaluation.

 **MINESTORMING**

Use the space below to record some of the great thoughts and ideas you've generated from reading Chapter Four.

_____
_____
_____
_____
_____
_____
_____
_____
_____
_____

CHAPTER 5

WebMAC Junior–2000: The Instrument

Introduction

The next several pages include the new *WebMAC Junior–2000* instrument, which is based on feedback from practitioners like you. As we described in Chapter Three, the new instrument covers all the basic information as the earlier versions, but takes less time to administer, uses less paper, and includes several slightly modified wordings of questions to improve comprehension. To further conserve on paper, you may not need to copy the instructions page if you read them aloud. This may be preferable anyway for very young students. This new instrument is becoming the most popular choice for teaching situations on the elementary level.

Those of you, however, who may be in the process of *designing* a Web site and are interested in putting together a focus group to review progress, may find the *WebMAC Junior Long Form* even more useful. The longer instrument has several additional items that focus on aesthetic concerns. A focus group or panel situation generally allows more time for evaluation, and children selected to participate in a focus group or panel may be more willing to take their time with a longer instrument. As mentioned earlier, you can find the instrument in Appendix D. Because it is a longer version, the scoring procedures are different. There are specific scoring sheets and grids that you must use with *WebMAC Junior Long Form*. These also are included in the Appendices following the instrument. Other than that, you can follow the same basic administration procedures as you would for *WebMAC Junior–2000*.

Don't forget that you can also find *WebMAC Middle* in Appendix C, including both the instrument and scoring sheets. You may find this version preferable if you are working with upper elementary or middle school children who might perceive the smiley faces as babyish. *WebMAC Middle* contains 24 items.

Chapter Objectives

By the end of Chapter Five, you should:
▶ be familiar enough with the instrument to administer it to your class.
▶ start to think of ways you can use *WebMAC Junior–2000* in a lesson designed to teach children evaluation skills using the World Wide Web.

WebMAC Junior—2000

(Arnone, M.P., & Small, R.V., 1999)

Name: _____ School: _____

Grade: _____ Date: _____

Web Site Address: _____

Instructions

Just like the judges who decide the winners in an art or science contest, you are one of the judges for this Web site. After reading each question, circle the face that best describes how you would rate this Web site. Remember that there are no right or wrong answers. First, try the example below.

Example

Did this Web site contain things that you are interested in?

If you circle the sad face ☹, it means that this Web site is really poor in this category. In other words, there is nothing in this Web site that is of interest to you. You give it the lowest score, which is 0 points. If you circle the face with no expression 😐 (just a straight line for the mouth), it means that this Web site is OK, but there's nothing special that interests you. If you circle the face with a small smile ☺, it means that this Web site is not the best, but it is good. If you circle the face with a big smile ☺, it means that this Web site is excellent—definitely one of the best Web sites you have seen when it comes to things that interest you. You give it 3 points, the highest score!

WebMAC Junior—2000

1. Was this an interesting or fun Web site to explore?

2. Could you read and understand most of the words that were used?

3. Was the information at this Web site believable? (Did it seem to be true?)

4. Was it easy to find your way around without getting lost?

5. Did the pictures, sounds, or videos make this Web site more interesting?

6. Was it easy to find what you needed at this Web site?

7. Did this Web site have links to other interesting or useful Web sites?

8. Did all the parts of this Web site work the way they should?

9. Were there lots of activities to do at this Web site?

10. Were the directions for using this Web site simple and clear?

11. Do you think this Web site sometimes adds new things to read about and do?

12. Did things like pictures, games, or videos *quickly* come up on the screen?

13. Did you like the colors and backgrounds used at this Web site?

14. Did you find enough of what you were looking for at this Web site?

☹ 😐 🙂 😃
0   1   2   3

15. Was what you found at this Web site useful to you?

☹ 😐 🙂 😃
0   1   2   3

16. Were there ways of getting help if you needed it at this Web site?

☹ 😐 🙂 😃
0   1   2   3

Would you like to visit this Web site again sometime? (✔) YES ☐ NO ☐

Is this a Web site that friends your age would like to visit? YES ☐ NO ☐

What did you like best about this Web site? Write in the space below.

_____

_____

What would make this Web site better? Write your ideas below.

_____

_____

COMING UP...

Hopefully, your students will enjoy being the judges for a Web site. They will be learning important evaluation skills at the same time. Once they have completed *WebMAC Junior–2000*, they may be wondering how to make sense of their responses. In Chapter Six, you will find the scoring devices your students can use to discover how their Web site(s) stacks up.

HIGHLIGHTS of Chapter Five

In Chapter Five, you were provided with the new *WebMAC Junior–2000* instrument. This instrument was modified from the longer form based on feedback from educators and a pilot study involving more than 500 students. The Appendices include the *WebMAC Junior Long Form*, which may be helpful to Web developers. *WebMAC Middle* is also included in the Appendices.

MINESTORMING

As you were reviewing *WebMAC Junior*, did you think of ways you might incorporate the instrument into your information literacy curriculum? Why not do some *minestorming* right now? Use the space below to record your ideas.

_____
_____
_____
_____
_____
_____
_____
_____
_____
_____

Chapter 6

Scoring *WebMAC* Junior–2000

Introduction

In this chapter, you will find everything you will need to score *WebMAC Junior–2000*, including tally sheets and grids for charting results.

Chapter Objectives

When you have completed Chapter Six, you will be able to:
▶ use the individual and class scoring forms in evaluating a Web site.
▶ use the grid to visually represent the results of a Web site evaluation.

Scoring Individually and As A Class

As you know from the administration directions, scores range from 0 to 3, as indicated below. When you pass out the scoring sheets, make sure that you have explained how these numbers relate to the smiley faces.

Older children may be capable of scoring their own evaluations while younger children will require the teacher or administrator to score. Using the reproducible scoring sheet provided in this chapter, have students add up all the odd-numbered items under Column A and all the even-numbered items under Column B. After the class has scored their individual evaluations, a general discussion could ensue with individual students describing their results.

Let's say each member of your class individually rated the same Web site. You could also take all the individual scores, average them, and come up with an overall class rating of the site. To make this quicker, use the class tally sheet and class plotting grid provided in this chapter. The class tally sheet and plotting grid include specific directions. You will also find that in Chapter Twelve, we have included overhead transparency masters; you can use these if you decide to tally and plot the scores in front of your class so that they can view the process.

Master for Copy Purposes

Name: _____ Grade: _____

WebMAC Junior—2000
(Arnone, M.P., & Small, R.V., 1999)

Individual Scoring Sheet

Instructions: Have your *WebMAC Junior–2000* with your filled in responses beside you. Using this scoring sheet, copy the score for each question next to the number of that question. Notice that odd-numbered questions are under Column A and even-numbered questions are under Column. Then add up the scores for each column.

A   **B**

1. _____   2. _____

3. _____   4. _____

5. _____   6. _____

7. _____   8. _____

9. _____   10. _____

11. _____   12. _____

13. _____   14. _____

15. _____   16. _____

TOTAL A: _____   **TOTAL B:** _____

WebMAC Junior—2000: Class Tally Sheet

Instructor Directions: Sometimes a group or entire class will evaluate the same Web site. If you would like to calculate their summary and average scores, you can use the tally sheet below to record each individual student's scores (up to 30 students) for **A** (*How Interesting*) and **B** (*How Well It Works*). Then, total and average each column and plot the class average scores on the "Class Rating of Web Site" scoring grid included in this chapter.

A	B
1. _____	1. _____
2. _____	2. _____
3. _____	3. _____
4. _____	4. _____
5. _____	5. _____
6. _____	6. _____
7. _____	7. _____
8. _____	8. _____
9. _____	9. _____
10. _____	10. _____
11. _____	11. _____
12. _____	12. _____
13. _____	13. _____
14. _____	14. _____
15. _____	15. _____
16. _____	16. _____
17. _____	17. _____
18. _____	18. _____
19. _____	19. _____
20. _____	20. _____
21. _____	21. _____
22. _____	22. _____
23. _____	23. _____
24. _____	24. _____
25. _____	25. _____
26. _____	26. _____
27. _____	27. _____
28. _____	28. _____
29. _____	29. _____
30. _____	30. _____

Total A Scores: _____   **Total B Scores:** _____

Average A Scores: _____   **Average B Scores:** _____

Plotting the Scores

Older children may appreciate a more visual representation of the scores. In upper elementary or middle schools, many children will understand a rudimentary graph. Provide them with a copy of the reproducible grid on page 79. Show them how to plot the score they gave the Web site according to the directions on the same page. On the graph, *Not Interesting–Very Interesting* represents the **Value** component, and *Works Well–Works Poorly* represents the **Expectation for Success** component. In the example below, the Web site rates in the average to high category for *how interesting* (20) but in the below average to low category for *how well it works* (7). This means that, in this young rater's opinion, the Web site has interest for him, but the designer(s) should try to improve the Web site to make it function better in the areas noted on the rater's evaluation form. You will find another example plotted on the following page.

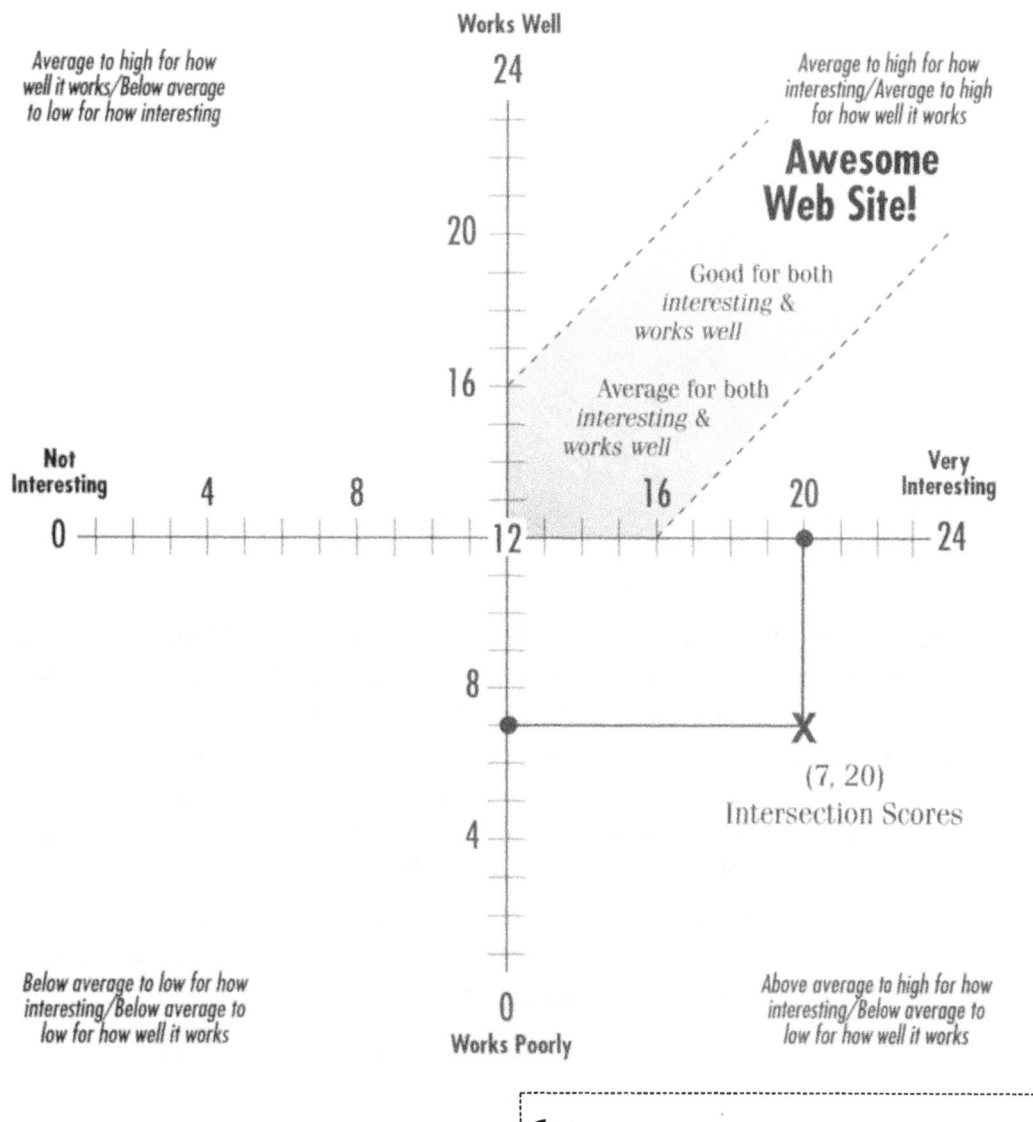

A Second Example

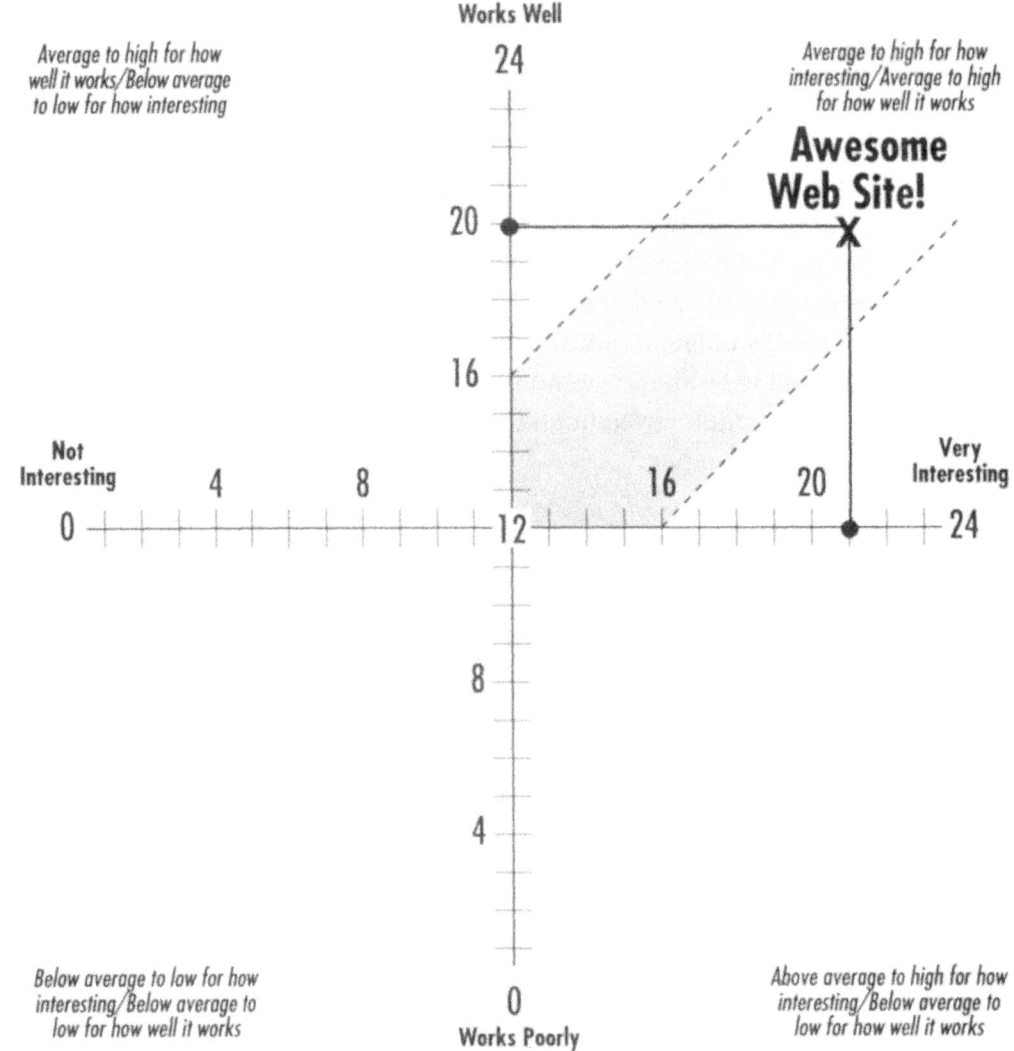

In the example above, the scores for *how interesting* (21) and *how well it works* (20) both fell into the upper right quadrant. Scores that fall into this quadrant represent a Web site that has been rated at least average or above on both dimensions. This particular example shows an even better result. As you can see, the intersection point of the two scores falls into the gray channel in the *Awesome Web Site* range. This means that the rater for this site felt the site was outstanding all the way around. Scores that land in the upper right quadrant can be average or good on one dimension and fall into the awesome range on the other. Both scores, however, must be 20 or above to have their intersection point fall into the *Awesome Web Site* range.

WebMAC Junior—2000
(Arnone, M.P., & Small, R.V., 1999)

Rate This Web Site!

Student Directions: On the grid, you will notice that the horizontal line is for the "How Interesting" score (the A score) and the vertical line is for the "How Well It Works" score (or the B score). Place a dot for the A score along the *Not Interesting–Very Interesting* line; place a dot for the B score along the *Works Well–Works Poorly* line. Then, draw straight lines to their point of intersection. Good Web sites will have both scores in the upper right section. An awesome Web site will have scores that fall in the extreme upper right section labeled *"Awesome Web Site!"*

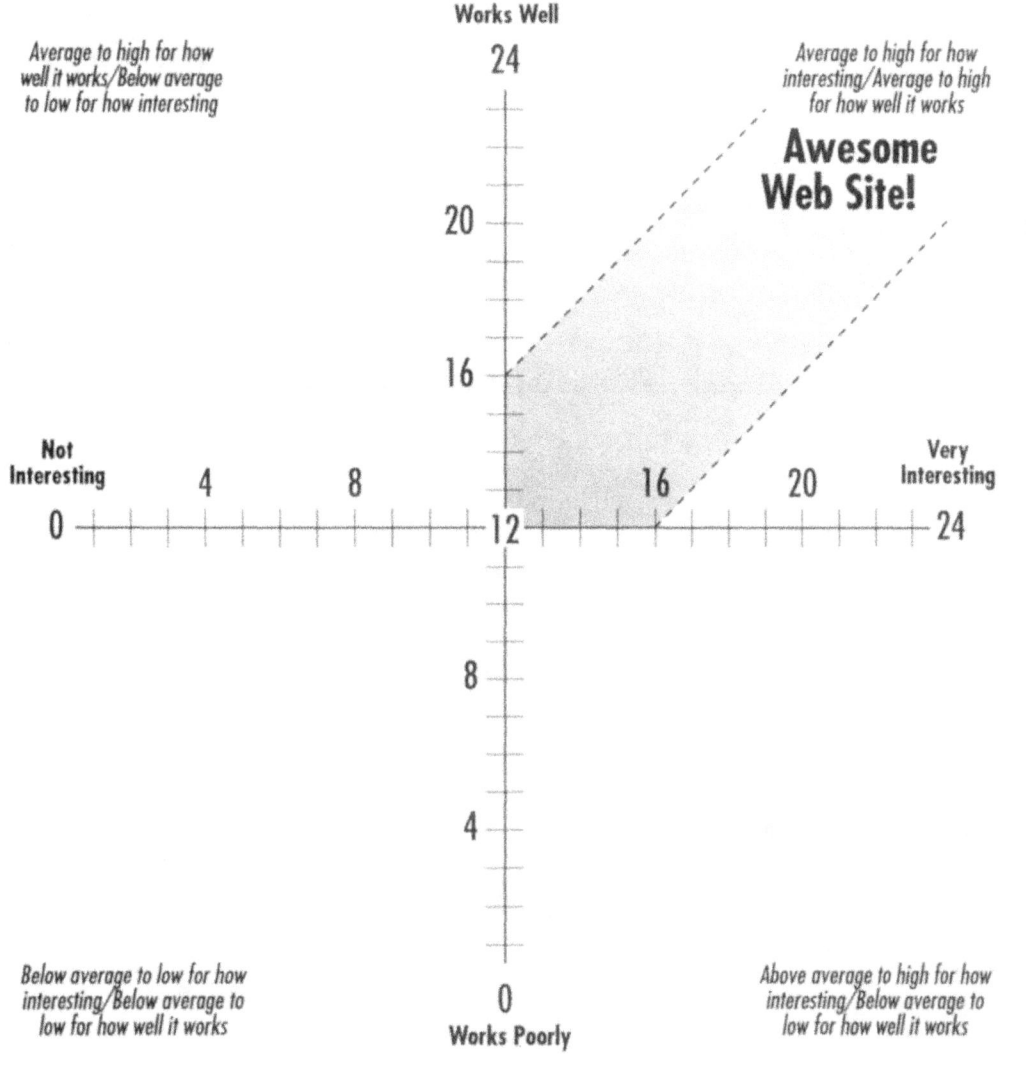

WWW MOTIVATION MINING: FINDING TREASURES FOR TEACHING EVALUATION SKILLS, GRADES 1-6 — CHAPTER 6: SCORING WEBMAC JUNIOR—2000

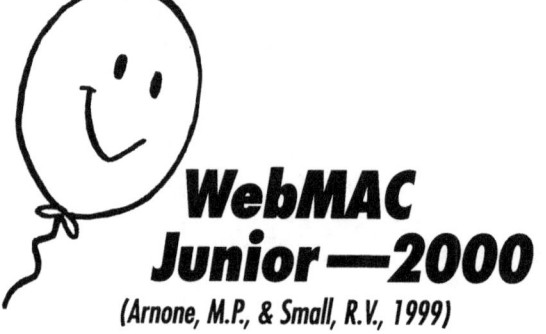

WebMAC Junior—2000
(Arnone, M.P., & Small, R.V., 1999)

Class Rating of Web Site

Instructor Directions: Use the results of the Class Tally Sheet and plot the average **A** (**Value** or *How Interesting*) and **B** (**Expectation for Success** or *How Well It Works*) scores on the grid below.

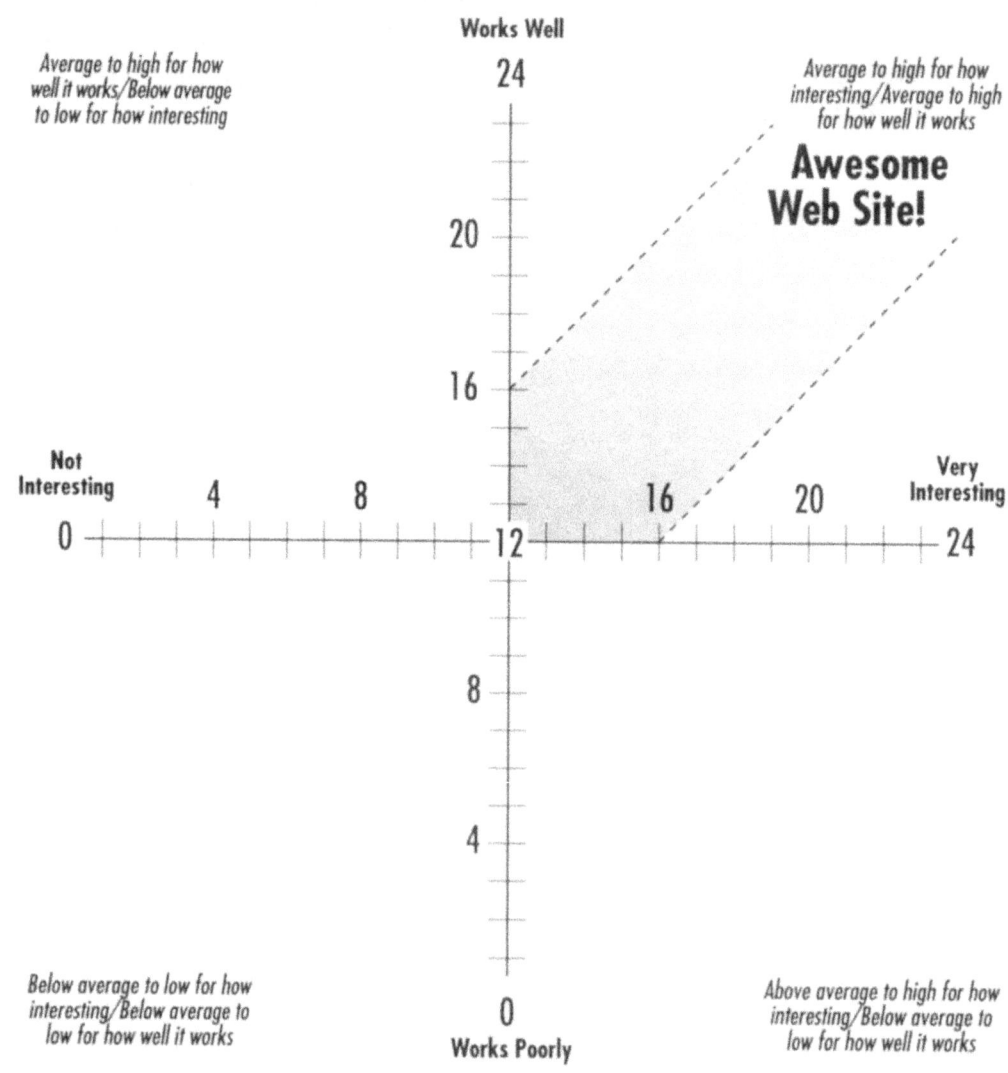

COMING UP...

That's it for scoring! In Chapter Seven, you will learn how to interpret the scores for your students.

HIGHLIGHTS of Chapter Six

In Chapter Six, scoring procedures for individual and class ratings of Web sites were explained. Reproducible individual scoring sheets as well as a class tally were provided. You also received instructions for visually representing the results of both individual and class ratings of a Web site on a graph.

 **MINESTORMING**

Any ideas? Jot them down below while they are still fresh in your mind.

_____
_____
_____
_____
_____
_____
_____
_____
_____
_____

Chapter 7

Interpreting Results

Introduction

Many of the educators who have used this instrument tell us that once students have explored how evaluation applies to Web resources and completed *WebMAC Junior–2000*, they begin asking "What do my scores mean?" Many times, interpreting scores is an enjoyable culminating activity for students in a unit on evaluation.

Chapter Objectives

By the end of Chapter Seven, you should be able to:
▶ model the process of interpreting scores to your students.
▶ explain what the **A** and **B** scores represent.
▶ provide examples to your students of Web site attributes that contribute to the *How Interesting* and *How Well It Works* scores.
▶ explain to students the relationship between the **A** and **B** scores and the overall Web site rating.
▶ discuss with your class the summary results of an evaluation in which each individual in the class has rated a particular Web site.

Explaining the Significance of the A and B Scores

While you understand how value and expectation for success contribute to a student's perception of a Web site, those terms are much too abstract to use with this age group. To help students in elementary grades understand the results of their evaluation, we recommend using the phrases *How Interesting* for the **Value** dimension and *How Well It Works* for the **Expectation for Success** dimension.

Once your students have tallied up their individual **A** and **B** scores, ask them to share their *How Interesting* scores for the Web site they are evaluating. Then do the same for the *How Well It Works* scores. Get a few scores for each dimension, and then refer to the score key, which you could display on an overhead or whiteboard. The scoring key is below.

Score Key

A (*How Interesting*)		**B** (*How Well It Works*)	
0-5	Poor	0-5	Poor
6-11	Below Average	6-11	Below Average
12-15	Average	12-15	Average
16-19	Good	16-19	Good
20-24	Excellent	20-24	Excellent

A and **B** scores that are both in the Excellent range will translate into an "Awesome Web Site," but we'll discuss that overall score later. First, students should have an understanding of the Web site attributes that contribute to each of these scores.

What Makes a Web Site Interesting and Valuable?

When discussing what contributes to the A score, it might be helpful to have students refer to the questions on *WebMAC Junior–2000*. Select the odd-numbered items since each of those relates to that score. For example, if you ask them to look at Question #1, it is obvious that this relates to how interesting they thought the site might be, even at first glance.

Explain that the *How Interesting* score also includes how valuable the site is to them. If the site does not have value to them, their interest would diminish. This score includes things like whether the site has good information that is accurate and credible. Question #3 refers to this quality: "Was the information on this Web site believable? (Did it seem to be true?)" You could ask your students what made them think that the information was believable. Was it because the author of the Web site was identified as an expert in his or her field? Was it because the Web site was sponsored by a trusted organization like the state or federal government? You would not expect them to stay interested in a Web site for long if they needed accurate information for a school project and they couldn't be sure they were getting it. You could also mention other things that contributed to the **A** score such as the usefulness of the information for the students' needs (Question #15) and how up-to-date the Web site is (Question #11).

What Makes a Web Site Work Well and Enjoyable

To help students understand the significance of the **B** score, have them refer to the even-numbered questions on *WebMAC Junior–2000*. Question #4 asks them how easy it was to find their way around the different parts of the Web site without getting lost. Explain to them that this has to do with *how well the Web site works*. If the Web site is not organized well or is difficult to navigate, they would be disappointed and may not even want to continue exploring the site. How quickly the pictures and other things came up on screen (Question #12) and whether all the parts (e.g., games, downloading) worked the way they should (Question #8) all relate to the **B** score. When things work the way they should in a Web site, the learner can expect to be successful in navigating through the site, linking to other resources, and quickly accessing information. This contributes to a feeling of satisfaction on the part of learners. If they are satisfied, they are likely to return at another time (YES/NO question following Question #16). Explain to students that these are important things to remember when evaluating a Web site or if they ever design their own Web sites.

Demonstrating How the **A** and **B** Scores Contribute to an Overall Rating

Once students understand the significance of each score, you can discuss how the two scores together contribute to the overall rating of the Web site. An excellent site does well on both scores. You can make this idea more concrete by asking questions like the following and leaving time in between to get responses from students:

> *"What if you found a Web site that had lots of interesting information that you could use for a project you were working on, that would be a good thing, right? BUT what if it wasn't easy to find that information on the Web site and everything took a real long time to get to, would that make you feel upset? Do you think you would stay at that Web site for very long if you couldn't get what you needed? How many of you would come back and visit that site some other time?... You see, a good Web site is interesting and has valuable information, AND it works the way it should."*

Plotting the two scores on the graph according to the directions in Chapter Six helps to illustrate how it takes good scores in both *How Interesting* and *How Well It Works* to have a high-quality Web site. Scores that are both above average will fall into the upper right quadrant of the graph. Two excellent scores will fall into the Awesome *Web Site* range. Plotting scores on the grid may be most effective for use in the upper elementary and early middle school grades. Most children in this age range enjoy the opportunity to visually represent their results.

Although an *Awesome Web Site* is one that scores generally high in all areas, it is important to explain that no Web site is perfect. There are always areas that could be improved. Furthermore, a Web site does not have to include lots of "bells and whistles" to be rated *Awesome*. For example, animations may or may not add to the motivational quality of a specific site. So-called "glitz" is not an essential criterion for a Web site to receive an *Awesome* rating. We have included a few visuals as reproducible overheads in Chapter 12. You might find these helpful when introducing some of the concepts.

Finally, you may want to interpret the results of the class overall. This helps to demonstrate to students that Web site revision shouldn't be made on the basis of one score. Often, it takes the work of a number of evaluators to make decisions when making modifications or changes to Web sites. Using the class tally and then plotting the average class score helps students to see how their individual input contributes to the larger evaluation. In Chapter Eight, you will see a good example of how a pair of educators used a school home page in an exercise designed to do just that.

COMING UP...

The *WebMAC* instruments have already been used by many educators across the country. In Chapter Eight, we interview some of them to give you ideas on how educators are making motivation mining on the World Wide Web work for them.

HIGHLIGHTS of Chapter Seven

Chapter Seven focused on how to help students interpret the results of their evaluation once they have finished scoring. It is important to make sure they understand the attributes of a Web site that contribute to the *How Interesting* and *How Well It Works* scores. They should also understand that it is necessary for a Web site to have strengths in both these categories to be considered for a high overall rating. Plotting scores on a grid helps students to visualize the results and works best with older children.

MINESTORMING

Before moving on to read how some of your colleagues are teaching evaluation skills using Web-based resources, take a moment and minestorm some of your own ideas for teaching this important information skill.

_____

_____

_____

_____

_____

_____

_____

_____

_____

_____

 **SELF-CHECK**

1) Describe three ways of using motivational assessment.

2) How can you as a teacher or LMS foster a positive attitude in your students regarding information exploration and evaluation?

3) How do you explain **Value** (V) and **Expectation for Success** (XS) in a way young students can understand?

4) What is the purpose of plotting scores on a grid?

5) What is one way you could discuss the attributes of a Web site that contribute to its rating?

6) In order for a Web site to be rated in the "Awesome Web Site" range, what two things are necessary?

Suggested Responses to Part II Self-Check

1) Describe three ways of using motivational assessment.

   As a teaching tool, a lesson-planning tool, and a research and development tool.

2) How can you as a teacher or LMS foster a positive attitude in your students regarding information exploration and evaluation?

   Model enthusiasm as you teach information skills to children.

3) How do you explain **Value** (V) and **Expectation for Success** (XS) in a way young students can understand?

   Explain V as "How interesting" and XS as "How well it (the Web site) works."

4) What is the purpose of plotting scores on a grid?

   So that students may have a visual representation of the overall rating of a Web site (not appropriate for the youngest students).

5) What is one way you could discuss the attributes of a Web site that contribute to its rating?

   Refer to the actual questions on WebMAC Junior–2000 as examples during the discussion.

6) In order for a Web site to be rated in the "Awesome Web Site" range, what two things are necessary?

   The Web site must have high scores in both "How Well It Works" and "How Interesting."

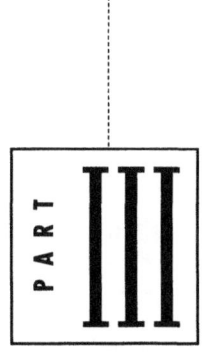

Panning for Web Gold

Chapter 8

A Treasure Chest of Ideas from Educators

Introduction

In preparing this book, we interviewed a number of educators and library media specialists to get their ideas on evaluation of Web resources and the importance of motivation. We also wanted to hear their insights on *WebMAC Junior* as we moved closer to the new *WebMAC Junior–2000*. They not only told us about the context in which they used *WebMAC Junior* (and in some cases *WebMAC Middle*), but they also shared some ideas for how they might use it in the future. We hope their stories will spark some ideas of your own.

Chapter Objectives

After reading Chapter 8, you should:
▶ understand how educators are using motivational assessment.
▶ be able to generate ideas for how you could use the *WebMAC* instruments in your school.

Gems and Nuggets from the "MasterMines"

Throughout this book, we have used the "mining" analogy with reference to motivation. It's fun and interesting to contrast such an old art with such new technology as the World Wide Web. Just as in "the ole days," when you run into a precious gem in *motivation mining*, you know it's the real article and not "fool's gold." Get ready to dig up plenty of the real articles in this chapter!

Kathy Schrock states that "teaching critical evaluation of Internet sites and information is best conducted when students have 'real' projects to do."[1] We agreed and asked some educators to describe how they taught their students to use *WebMAC Junior* and *WebMAC Middle* to strike Web gold. Here are some of their "gems"—accounts of what they did and how they did it. We also provide some of their actual lesson plans (which you may want to adapt) in Appendix B. Interspersed with the gems that follow are a few nuggets that we have found along the way.

Our first gem comes from a very creative team at Killearn Lakes Elementary School in Tallahassee, Florida. They are Roberta Mann, Media Specialist, and Barbara "Bobbie" Buckingham. Bobbie was a teacher for 20 years and she presently teaches math skills to gifted children. Through her collaboration with Roberta, she also teaches media literacy, something that Roberta recently introduced at this school. Roberta has been a media specialist for 27 years. They decided to use *WebMAC Junior* in conjunction with teaching evaluation skills to more than 175 fifth grade students. Students had little prior exposure to any kind of evaluation of Internet resources. "Their skills are not refined yet. They are very new at this [evaluation]," said Bobbie. This would mean that gaining and sustaining student interest would be critical, as would making the assignments meaningful in the students' minds.

Bobbie started with Web sites that were on the school's home page. The students evaluated a common Web site that was appropriate to Bobbie's curriculum. They also reviewed the school's home page itself. This latter assignment resulted in a great deal of student interest, largely due to the motivational strategies that Bobbie used to enhance the importance (meaningfulness) of the assignment. For example, she told the students that the results of their evaluation of the school's home page would be shared with "Ms. Mann" (who is responsible for the school's Web site), and that modifications and changes based on their feedback could occur. This definitely increased the relevance of the assignment, and students felt empowered by their responsibility. Students took the assignment "in a serious frame of mind" according to Bobbie.

WebMAC Junior also related well to Bobbie's use of it in conjunction with math skills. Each of the seven classes of fifth graders filled in the evaluation booklets and did a class tally. Thus, each class had a pair of scores for "how interesting" (value) and "how well it works" (expectation for success). She then took all seven class tallies and averaged each pair of scores to come up with one overall rating for the school's Web site, more than 175 fifth graders! She plotted this overall score on the grid. Each student could see firsthand how his or her individual input contributed to the larger school evaluation.

Another motivational strategy that Bobbie used prior to actually conducting the evaluation was to give the students a practice session ahead of time to become familiar with the instrument and how to use it to evaluate a Web site. Practice serves to build confidence, which is important when students are just learning information skills.

Both Roberta and Bobbie felt that an abbreviated form of the *WebMAC Junior* instrument would be useful since schools generally have a limited copy budget. In fact, they actually shrank down the instrument in order to use it with such a large group. Their comments contributed to the development of the new *WebMAC Junior*. Roberta and Bobbie have plans to use the new *WebMAC Junior* in conjunction with several other assignments. Roberta plans to offer a workshop to her colleagues on evaluating web resources and will incorporate the overheads supplied in this book in Part IV: Sharing the Wealth.

NUGGET Have students evaluate a specific Web site and ask a parent or other adult to evaluate the same Web site. Discuss the similarities and differences in the results.

 Dr. Barbara Boone Buescher is a Media Specialist at Ravenscroft School, an independent school in Raleigh, North Carolina. Her doctorate is in English education. She also has experience working on the state level evaluating commercial software to support the curriculum. She was on contract with the North Carolina Department of Public Instruction to write many reviews which were included in the *School Library Journal* in its CD-ROM software review column. At Ravenscroft, Barbara is responsible for the PreK-5 information skills curriculum but, so far, she has used *WebMAC Junior* only for the fourth graders. She has a full-time assistant and occasional parent volunteers. There are four fourth grade classes with a total of 72 students.

When Barbara asked students what kind of information resources they could use to complete research, they often mentioned books, magazines, and the "computer." One of her challenges, she said, was to get students to think of the computer as the conduit for information from a variety of sources, as opposed to the source itself. The fourth grade students she described had varying degrees of experience exploring the Internet at home and until recently had little or no experience on the Internet in school. While she believes in giving students choices, she doesn't encourage them to freely explore at school. She commented that there is neither enough time nor enough computers. She also told us that evaluation is important, as "children need to get an early critical perspective." She chose *WebMAC Junior* because it allowed students to look at a Web site in a structured but appealing way.

Barbara provided us with a different example of how *WebMAC Junior* could be used. It is a self-directed activity in a learning station, one of six centers through which students rotate during media center visits. Classes of 18 fourth graders rotate in groups of three, through six different learning centers, with groups visiting all of the stations over the six-week period. Each class visit lasts 45 minutes. Other stations include free reading, geography software, and areas where students can work on skills like putting books in order on the shelf and then shelving books with the help of an assistant. There is also "Regional Round-Up" in which students read picture books and identify regional characteristics in the books, based on their study of U.S. geography.

At the learning station, three computers are presently dedicated to *WebMAC Junior*. Barbara bookmarked four to six possible Web sites students may choose from. They are expected to review the selected Web site and evaluate it using the *WebMAC* instrument. Her goal is for students to "be able to look at [the Web site] in a structured way so that they might be able to compare it with another Web site down the road, or to be able to compare it with another one that perhaps someone else in their group evaluated." When a student arrives at a *WebMAC* computer, he or she selects a site from the bookmark. A blue folder sits beside the computer. On the outside of the folder, the students are greeted with: "Welcome to *WebMAC* Internet Analysis. Here's what to do. Your mission is to rate this Web site according to the smiley face checklist...." To conserve money on copying, Barbara has laminated the *WebMAC Junior* instrument and instructions, which remain in the blue folder after the student finishes. The students place their responses on a separate answer sheet. The activity is not totally self-directed, as Barbara and her assistant circulate among the six workstations giving students personal attention as needed. Students need basic navigational tips when exploring links, she commented. "They tend to just click, click, click," she said, sometimes winding up someplace without a clue of how they got there or whether it fits in with their search plan.

Barbara plans to consolidate the results of the *WebMAC Junior* exercise. "I think the kids will be interested in the follow-up from [*WebMAC Junior* evaluations], and I could show a graph or maybe even get some of them to help me make one. I think they are doing it in computer and math now. There are a lot of opportunities for pulling this into all different content areas." Barbara has not yet collaborated with a teacher to use *WebMAC Junior* as part of a curricular project; however, that's in her plans. She is considering using *WebMAC Junior* again next term. She feels that if the kids practice using it to develop evaluation skills, that they will be better prepared and more adept at evaluating potential sources when they later approach a large curricular project. Like several others, Barbara said she would also appreciate a shorter instrument for *WebMAC Junior*. With as many students as she has, the cost of copying can be high and a shorter instrument would also help with the time issue.

We asked Barbara if she had any other ideas she could share with her colleagues that could serve as a motivational strategy to excite kids about using evaluation skills. She came up with two excellent ones. The first could be used if you are concerned that your students may not be quite ready to evaluate a Web site on their level (e.g., they lack experience in exploring the Internet). For this situation, Barbara suggested selecting a Web site targeted at much younger children. "You could show them Web sites that are designed for much younger children if you made that overt. You might say to students: 'Think about your kindergarten buddies... you're older students and we want you to decide if this Web site would be a good one for your younger brothers or sisters'... You could start them [older students] with a simpler Web site." We thought this was a great idea for getting budding young evaluators off to a positive start. As an added bonus, students are "gaining experience in considering another's perspective," said Barbara.

Her second idea is similar to peer tutoring but with a different spin. Barbara suggested identifying several students who could work with students in an earlier grade as the "experts" showing them how to use *WebMAC Junior*. The younger students would look up to their older counterparts, and the tutors would feel a sense of leadership. This strategy would definitely accommodate some of the individual differences we find in students. For example, students who have a high need for affiliation or for leadership opportunities would be great candidates for Barbara's strategy. She added that it also may help in terms of student behavior and maintaining focus if students know they might be spotted for this prestigious assignment. "It might also give students a hook for maybe approaching [learning evaluation skills] a little more seriously."

Barbara said something else that made a lot of sense. She commented that it is not just the elementary students who are naturally still new to all of this. "We, as teachers and librarians, are also still learning... about how kids use and adapt to technology. We need to be observant of that so that we can teach around it." She is right. When it comes to the World Wide Web, we may all be on a learning curve for some time to come! (Actually, that's a good thing, don't you think?)

Evaluate several other classes or school Web sites to help guide students as they design their own Web sites.

Deb Christensen is a graduate student in the Master of Library Science program at Syracuse University's School of Information Studies. This next precious gem is a result of her internship project, which she developed and implemented with the help of LMS Glenda House of the Lake Street Elementary School in Chittenango, New York. Deb enjoyed combining forces with Glenda on this lesson, and she also places a high value on collaboration between teachers and LMSs. "I think [collaboration is] very important," she said. It can add a lot to the classroom studies as well as to library time. And it's really good for the students, too, to develop their information skills across the board."

Lake Street Elementary is a K-2 school, but Glenda believes that grade level not too young to start teaching kids evaluation skills, even the youngest ones. She said:

> *"I don't think kindergartners are too young to train to be critical thinkers [and] evaluators of information resources. I would not use that exact language with them when I talk to them about different resources that I am sharing with them. I am always asking them 'What do you like about this book?' 'What don't you like about this book?' With my second graders, I get into bigger vocabulary words such as **resources** and **evaluating** and **critical thinking**. I think that being critical evaluators of Web sources is just as important as print sources, probably more, as this is what these young children will be using the most as they get older."*

Deb's lesson using *WebMAC Junior* worked very well in achieving her overall goal of having students begin discussing the evaluation of resources by practicing with books and then a Web site. We thought you might appreciate reviewing Deb's detailed lesson plan, so we've included it in the Appendices. In the next few paragraphs, we will discuss it in general terms.

Deb and Glenda decided to use *WebMAC Junior* in the context of a larger two-part lesson on evaluation. The school had just been wired, and the second graders had little in-school experience on the Internet thus far. The strategy they used is an excellent one from a motivational perspective. They started by evaluating books and then the next week they evaluated a Web site. "I think that when asking [second graders] to use a new tool, it is best to start off slowly with something they can relate to easily," said Glenda. The books represented the "familiar" to the students while the Web represented the "unfamiliar." Building on the familiar is an excellent way of increasing student confidence when introducing something that is new or at least not as familiar.

In planning this lesson, Deb came up with an outstanding idea. She adapted *WebMAC Junior* to use as an evaluation instrument for books! It really got students into the whole concept of evaluation (with the familiar book format) before introducing Web site evaluation. Her adapted instrument is also included with her lesson plan in Appendix B. We call it *BookMAC*! Here is Deb's account of one example from the first week of the lesson plan, which started with book evaluation:

> *"Glenda held up different preselected books which had the titles and covers concealed. These particular books were selected based on Glenda's knowledge of the students who we would be working with. She anticipated which books the students would choose with the covers or titles concealed and also which books the students would want once the covers and titles were revealed.*

> *She asked the students which book they would choose if they could take one of the books out that day. The first two books were a world atlas and Santa's New Suit by Mike Lester (illustrator). The students were eager to take out the larger book thinking that it would be better simply because of its size. They dismissed the smaller book as not being as good or interesting as the larger book. Glenda asked the students to explain their choices and the responses for selecting the larger book ranged from 'bigger is better' to 'it has more information in it.' Glenda then showed the students what the books actually were. Santa's New Suit is a student favorite, and they all wanted to take that book out instead of the atlas once they saw what it was."*

They did a similar exercise with a second set of books. The students were able to clearly see that there is more to making judgments about books than just looking at the size, cover, or other superficial elements. This led nicely into a discussion of what types of things they should look for when selecting a book. They discussed how easy or difficult to read the words were, the type of information in the book, how up-to-date the information was, and whether they knew about or enjoyed a particular author. The students were then allowed to select a book of their choice (from a pre-selected group of books). The books were short and the students had some time to review or complete their reading. Following this, the students used Deb's adapted brief instrument to evaluate their book selections. The lesson concluded with a short discussion of the kinds of things they would be looking for in the books they might select for a classroom project they were working on.

Now, on to *WebMAC Junior*! Deb pre-loaded the Zoobooks Web site on the computers in the lab the following week. Deb and Glenda refreshed the students about the book evaluations they had done the week before. They then introduced the notion of evaluating a Web site and compared it to evaluating books like they had already done. They told the students they had selected the Web site because the second graders were working on an animal report in their classroom and might find some useful information on the site. Deb recounted how she proceeded with the lesson:

> *"I asked the students to go to the computers and start looking at the Web site. I took them through a few pages of the site and then allowed them time to explore the site on their own. After they had spent between 15-20 minutes navigating the site, I handed out the WebMAC Junior evaluation forms and discussed how they were similar to the forms they had filled out last week. I read the directions to the students and they started to fill out WebMAC Junior while they were looking at the Web site."*

Some students had problems with a couple of words like "information" and "improved," which Deb needed to explain. She also needed to reinforce that there were no right or wrong answers to *WebMAC Junior*. That said, she felt they enjoyed the assignment and playing, as she called it, "the role of critic." She also believes that being able to give their stamp of approval or saying what they like or don't like gives the kids the chance to feel they have a little power over something.

It's always interesting to discover what one would do differently if they had the chance to do it (whatever) again. So, what would Deb do differently if she had the chance to do her internship project again? We'll let Deb speak for herself.

> *"If I were to do this evaluation again, I would try to spend more time getting the students familiar with the Internet and navigating a Web site. I would also try to use WebMAC Junior more than once so that the students would become familiar with using it and would feel more comfortable. Perhaps, by using the form more than once and discussing the results, the student would accept that there were no right or wrong answers. They could also compare their ratings on different sites. It would be interesting to select more than one site on the same topic to see how the students compare them. Overall, it was a very interesting lesson and a good introduction to evaluation for the students."*

Glenda continues to use *WebMAC Junior* with other students and said they are really enjoying it. She believes that her own enthusiasm and motivation helps to motivate her students. She also is starting to pair up students to work on a Web site so they will start to see that they can have different opinions than their teammate. If they can't agree on a "face," she said, " ...It brings them to a much higher level of discussion without them actually realizing it."

Getting back to using books as a catalyst for evaluating electronic resources. . . Glenda sometimes slips in a book that may not be quite as good in some way as another and encourages the children to discuss it. She did this with several books on space. While one student liked a particular book because it had "good" information, another disapproved because, as she paraphrased the child's words, "It didn't talk about the new Hubble space telescope!" In that young evaluator's own way, he was saying that the book just wasn't "current" enough for him. You might want to try this approach with evaluating Web sites!

NUGGET Compare and discuss evaluations of the same Web site by different classes within the school, or compare and discuss evaluations of different Web sites by the same class.

Linda Zuber is a master of library science student at Syracuse University. She was also a participant in our 1998 Summer Workshop, where she was first introduced to *WebMAC Junior*. She loved it and wanted to find a way to use it in her elementary internship. Linda worked with Betsy Carnevale, an LMS from Durhamville (New York) Elementary School, on this next gem. In fact, we will be giving you highlights of two lessons that Linda shared with us. One of them is actually quite humorous. Let's start with that one!

Linda created a lesson for sixth grade students with the broad goal of having students realize that Web pages have to be examined critically for both accuracy and authenticity. Her specific objectives included having students evaluate how factual, current, and easy the Web site was to navigate, in addition to evaluating the authors' credibility. Here is where it gets funny. She had the students visit a Web site that was discussed on LM_NET (listserv) as a possibility for using in conjunction with teaching evaluation skills. The site was developed by Ken Umbach on "growing Velcro™" in California. She told her students she wanted them to evaluate the site. At first, the students seemed to think that the "Velcro-growing" Web site was legitimate. "We went on and on talking about what they liked and what they didn't like [about the Web site]," said Linda. "And it took [almost] the whole class period before they finally said, 'How do we know if this is true?'" Bingo!

At this point, Linda wrote on the whiteboard the letters F, A, C, and E. As the students offered their opinions, Linda would fill out the word for the mnemonic as each concept was discussed. The acronym "F. A. C. E." stood for *factual, author, current,* and *easy.* "Finally," Linda said, "a student offered that we really didn't know if this Web site was 'accurate' or provided the right 'facts.' She was outraged that they might have been SCAMMED! The other students were also shocked that they could have been scammed by a Web site. They decided to check the facts about *growing Velcro* using a reference book in the LMC." For Linda and her colleagues, it was interesting (and a bit amusing) to observe just how trusting students can be. According to Linda, her students could not believe that there was actually anything up on the Web that was totally wrong. And she paraphrased their sentiments with "And *WHO* would do something like that?" When she asked her students why they thought she might have shown them such a Web site, one responded, "Maybe to teach us we have to look hard at these Web sites?" That, of course, was the right answer!

In conjunction with her lesson plan, Linda adapted *WebMAC Junior* to work with her mnemonic "F.A.C.E.," and we were duly impressed. We think you might like to use it in your lab or LMC. Simply copy the two sides, cut out and paste together, laminate, and voila—you have a handy little learning aid to sit by your computers—compliments of Linda.

Let's F.A.C.E. It....

We've got to LOOK critically at Web pages!

Here's an easy way to remember what to think about:

Factual? (How do you know?)

Author? (What do you know about the author?)

Current? (When was the Web page last updated?)

Easy? (How easy was it to find your way around?)

For more questions you should ask yourself when you are thinking about using a Web site for homework or a school project, turn this card over.

Let's F.A.C.E. It....

Questions to ask when you look at a Web page:

Factual
- Is the information factual?
- Can you prove the information to be true?
- Does some information contradict information you found elsewhere?

Author
- Can you tell what author or organization made the Web page?
- Do you feel the author knows a lot about the topic?
- Is there information about the author?
- Is there a way to contact the author?

Current
- Is there a date on the page that tells you when it was last updated?
- Does it matter if the information is up-to-date?

Easy
- Does the layout of the Web page make it easy to use?
- Would it be easier to get this information from other references or resources?
- Does this page take a long time to load?
- Does the Web page have links to other information?
- If you go to another page on the site, can you get back to the main page easily?

From Arnone & Small (1999), *WWW Motivation Mining: Finding Treasures for Teaching Evaluation Skills*

Adapted from *WebMAC Junior* by Linda Zuber
Linworth Publishing

Looking for ideas to reinforce and expand students' understanding of the Dewey Decimal System? That was one of Linda's goals for another lesson she presented to fifth grade students. Additionally, she wanted her students to understand that "they can and should evaluate Web sites for accuracy, relevance, and ease of use." She found a student-created site called "'Do We' Really Know Dewey?" If you're interested, we have included Linda's lesson plan and student question sheet for that lesson in Appendix B.

Kathy Sommers is the library media specialist at West Point (New York) Elementary School, a Pre-K-Grade 4 school. Kathy had already planned a research unit for the third graders in her school when she discovered *WebMAC Junior*. "This is one of those projects that evolved," she said. "I had already started it when I read your article on *WebMAC* in *School Library Media Activities Monthly*, and I thought 'Oh, that sounds like the perfect conclusion to this lesson!'"

We asked her why she thought that Web site evaluation was important to teach her students, and she replied, "I believe that when elementary school students see something on a computer, they tend to take it at face value. At this level, children have rarely developed the ability to discriminate effectively."

Kathy's unit was designed to coincide with Black History Month, so the entire school was focused on this event. The students were required to compare information from two different sources and select facts on a specified topic (an African American who had been on one of the U.S. commemorative stamps). The sources they had to use were a print encyclopedia and a Web site featuring black Americans who had been on commemorative stamps. <http://www.library.advanced.org/10320/stamps.htm>.

"We have an in-house post office system called 'Wee Deliver,' sponsored by the U.S. Postal Service," Kathy explained. "One of the primary reasons the school adopted the program was so kids could develop their writing skills by writing letters to each other and to teachers." The main purpose of this project was to discover who the people on the stamps were and why they were chosen to appear on commemorative stamps, and then [for students] to use the facts they had gathered to support their nomination of that person to be on a West Point School stamp. After all the classes had turned in their nominations, a panel of external judges selected 20 nominees to be on stamps.

"Rather than having the same students who researched the person design the stamp, I gave their nomination information to groups of four to five other students who were charged with designing that person's stamp," she continued. If the nomination did not provide enough information to allow them to design a representative stamp, they became aware of the need to do additional research to fill the gaps. Again, when all designs were submitted, judges selected the 20 stamp designs.

At the conclusion of this portion of the project, a timeline display was arranged, which ran down the hall, displaying the 20 winning stamp designs with the winning nominations. It was at this point that Kathy saw the article about *WebMAC Junior* and thought, "Wow! This would be great!"

She told us, "This worked so well! When I started the unit, the objectives were that we were going to research and compare information from the print encyclopedias and the Web site, using the facts they would find to support an opinion. Now the project expanded in a new direction."

Students were given the opportunity to explore the Web site further because the only portion they had used was the bios that they printed out. Now they went back and checked out other parts of the Web site to see what else they could find—recipes, crafts, crossword puzzles, and so forth. Each group found different things.

"Then we came back together and talked about their discoveries before we did the *WebMAC*," she said. We talked about the Web site and about what had happened while they were doing research. For example, during the research portion there was a printing problem. If the information was one page long, it printed beautifully. But if it was two pages, page one printed out twice. So students had to take notes for everything more than one page long. They felt cheated—no one else had to do it that way—and frustrated. When they were taking notes, no one else could use the computer (they have only five computers). *WebMAC* provided great closure to our month-long project."

After refreshing their memories and sharing ideas, students worked in pairs. Kathy mused, "I think the kids thought it was interesting to think about some of these things (evaluation items). I heard them talking with their partners. One might feel strongly about something, and the other [might] not, but they had to reach a consensus. I don't think they thought consciously about those factors before using the *WebMAC*. They are more enthusiastic about doing research with something that does not appear to be dull or dry, so if you can hook them and get them interested in the site, they are more enthusiastic. *WebMAC* gave them specifics to look for and consider."

Kathy used a highly motivational approach to the assignment; she made it fun! "When I presented the project, I presented it as a contest—I don't think they ever really realized they were doing research," she said. "They were so excited when their nominee was chosen because they felt ownership. And they were happy for the designers who were chosen, even if wasn't their nominee. It worked so well and they were so pleased."

Then came the scoring. "We did class tallies of the evaluation results. All four classes' scores were pretty close together. It worked! I did not notice a great variance in individual responses. I'm considering sending feedback to the Web site's designers."

Whenever you can create a learning experience with a real-world application, you will increase relevance, and, hence, student motivation. Kathy found a way to do just that. "Soon after, I used what we learned from *WebMAC* again with a trial subscription to an online reference service. I told the kids we would evaluate the site to determine if they would want to spend our money on it for research. We talked again about features on the instrument. Then they worked in small groups to look up the person they had researched for their stamp using the trial software. Their conclusion was NO; only about half of them could find any information about the people they had researched before, and for the people who were able to find it, they decided the information on the site was not as useful as the other Web site or the encyclopedia. They were very adamant about their opinions.

"It was amazing. They were able to remember a lot of items from the instrument, even though we weren't using it. I think that because they had worked in pairs and had to discuss it that made it stick in their mind more. They had to defend their opinion to their partner. I think this exercise will change the way they look at Web sites."

Kathy would like to use *WebMAC Junior* again with this same group next year as fourth graders. "I thought the instrument was very well done. Kids are just not accustomed to thinking about who put a Web site together, and they tend to accept whatever's there even if it is not that useful to them. *WebMAC Junior* was just what I was looking for, and it worked very well with this particular project."

Remember the enthusiastic group of LMSs we were lucky enough to discover in Central Bucks County Elementary Schools in Pennsylvania? They were the ones who piloted the first 16-item *WebMAC Junior* instrument with more than 500 students! In Chapter Three, we discussed their pilot testing and feedback. With the feedback from that pilot study, we made a few more refinements before presenting *WebMAC Junior–2000* in this book. Now, in this "last but certainly not least" gem, we'll highlight one Bucks County LMS who used *WebMAC Junior* in a different way.

If you don't have enough computers to go around, there are always other options, according to Melissa Yates from Buckingham Elementary School. She used *WebMAC Junior* as a group activity with 80 second and third graders (we will focus on the third grade). With only one computer wired to the Internet and a digital projector, she explored a Web site with each class. Every child, however, was given his or her own evaluation form. "I told them clearly that 'I don't want to know what your neighbor thinks. I want to know what you think,'" Melissa explained. How do you get kids to maintain their own personal judgments while working in a group situation? "It really works well," said Melissa, "if you sit down with them ahead of time and talk about it." She used a creative approach to help her students understand that it is all right for everyone to have their own opinions and to make their own judgments.

She started on a very basic level holding up two toy screwdrivers. One was a monochromatic blue and flimsy. The other was brightly colored red and yellow, and solidly made. "Here are two screwdrivers," she said, "Which one do you think my son prefers?" Her students know all about her son, Timmy, since there is a picture of him in the LMC, and many were quick to respond that the two-year-old would certainly like the colorful yellow and red screwdriver the most. One student also mentioned that her son would like it because it was "sturdier." She told them they were probably right about Timmy's preference, but that not everyone would make the same choice. Everyone has his or her own preferences or choices. She then moved up to books.

Melissa showed the students three books each of which discussed penicillin. One was an ancient book called *Penny the Medicine Maker*. Another was called *A Hundred Greatest Medical Discoveries*, and the last was called *Mistakes That Worked*. She read them portions of the *Penny* book, followed by articles from the other two. Here is how she explained what happened.

> *"I said to them, 'There are no wrong answers, here. Any answer that you give will be correct. If you were going to write down information about penicillin, which of these books would you choose?' One kid said, 'I would use* A Hundred Greatest Medical Discoveries.*' I said, 'Fine, how many of you agree with that one?' Another said, 'I would read* Penny The Medicine Maker, *but I would add another book in because that one does not have enough facts in it.' 'OK, how many of you would do that? How many of you would use all three?' And we got to the point where we were talking about how each person has their own taste and their own opinion. I am the kind of person who loves things kind of tongue-and-cheek. So, for me,* Mistakes That Work *is the most attractive title. For your serious student,* A Hundred Greatest Medical Discoveries *is the most attractive title. For the kid who wants to clown around,* Penny the Medicine Maker *is the favorite. And it was interesting to see how they divided up."*

With the children feeling comfortable about making their own judgments, Melissa introduced them to *WebMAC Junior* and a Web site about butterflies. "From that discussion," she said, "we moved on to the actual [*WebMAC Junior*] form. I wanted to read it with them. Most of them could read but there are a couple that I knew couldn't. Then we moved over to the table and I put the projector on and we looked at Question #1. In the third grade case, we looked at the front page of the butterfly site. I ran down the whole first page. I said, 'Now, answer Question 1.' So they answered Question 1. Then I said to them, 'OK, where do you want to go?' and I let the children select where in the Web site we went."

Melissa found that working with the children in a group situation was successful. Plus, they loved the idea that they were helping to pilot test the new *WebMAC Junior*. "It gives them a feeling of participating; it makes them feel that they are valuable... and that they have an opinion that matters," Melissa commented. The Web site the third graders evaluated wasn't the most exciting, however—that is, until they got to the section on "Frequently Asked Questions About Butterflies." After going through the usual types of questions you might expect, things livened up a bit for the children. "Then, we got to 'Do butterflies go to the bathroom?' They loved it," explained Melissa. "Butterflies do not go to the bathroom. Did you know that?" she asked us. Well, actually we *didn't* know that, did you? Apparently, they do all their eating when they're caterpillars and excrete constantly then. When they become butterflies, they stop. Suddenly, the site went from fairly boring to pretty interesting. Melissa describes the exchange this way.

> *"They were stunned. First of all, they were stunned that I would actually discuss bathrooms with them. They were stunned that butterflies didn't go to the bathroom. Then, two questions down—'Do they have teeth?' Two hands went up. Turns out they do. They have opposable tooth mandibles. And they said, 'We didn't know that.' Well, I only learned that two days ago! So, finally [the site] was enjoyable."*

If you are wondering how these third graders rated the butterfly site, they were fairly consistent in their scoring. It certainly didn't achieve the Awesome Web Site rating, but it was at least in the above average range. We wonder if, without those two attention-getting "frequently asked" questions, the site might have scored even lower! In addition to learning about a great option for using *WebMAC Junior*, interviewing Melissa was a lot of fun.

The "Awesome Web Site" Award (AWArd)

Would your students like to share your *Awesome Web Site* discoveries with other educators or students? The authors invite entire classes of students (grades 1-6) to nominate their favorite curriculum-related Web sites for the *Awesome Web Site Award (AWArd)*. More information on the *AWArd* and how to submit a nomination is available on our Web site at <www.MotivationMining.com>. You can also reproduce the *AWArd* nomination form provided in Chapter Twelve.

 **COMING UP...**

In Chapter Nine, we'll explore some other ways that the *WebMAC* instruments are being used.

 **ENDNOTES**

[1] K. Schrock, "Evaluation of World Wide Web Sites: An Annotated Bibliography." *ERIC Digest*, June 1998. (ED-IR-98-02)

 **HIGHLIGHTS of Chapter Eight**

There are many creative ways to teach young children evaluation skills and to reinforce their importance. In Chapter Eight, we featured a number of excellent ideas that practitioners have actually used.

MINESTORMING

Did Chapter Eight give you any ideas for lessons you might develop to teach your students evaluation skills? What about ideas for using *WebMAC Junior–2000* or *WebMAC Middle*? Write them down below, even if they are still quite vague. They may trigger other ideas when you come back to them later.

_____
_____
_____
_____
_____
_____
_____
_____
_____
_____

Chapter 9

Other Great Ideas for Using the *WebMAC* Instruments

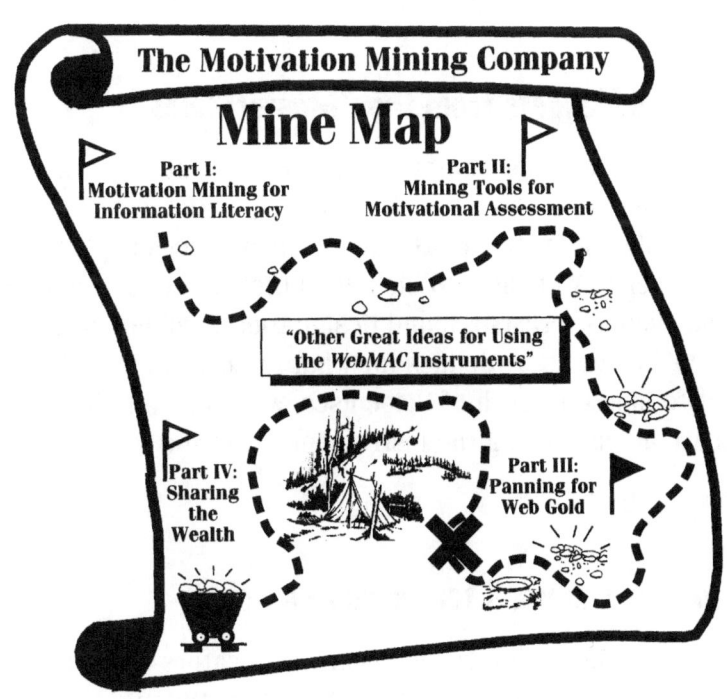

Introduction

In Chapter Eight, we presented some stories about how teachers and library media specialists have been using the "Junior" and "Middle" instruments for teaching critical evaluation skills to their students. In this chapter, we focus on other ways that the instruments could and have been used. For example, we interviewed a library media specialist who is also studying for her master's degree. She is using the instrument to evaluate Web sites for inclusion in her own "electronic portfolio." The instruments also make valuable lesson-planning tools to be shared among colleagues. We'll even tell you how one of the earlier versions of *WebMAC Junior* was used in research for a children's television program's Web site! As you read this chapter, think about other ways you can envision using the *WebMAC* instruments. As you think of them, you might want to write them down on Chapter Nine's Minestorming page.

Chapter Objectives

When you have finished Chapter Nine, you should:
▶ have an awareness of the variety of uses for *WebMAC Junior–2000* and *WebMAC Middle*.
▶ feel inspired to think of and try new ideas of your own!

More Gems and Nuggets from the "MasterMines"

As we mentioned in Chapter Three, there are other uses for the *WebMAC* instruments beyond a tool for teaching students critical evaluation skills. For example, the instruments may be used as lesson-planning tool to help educators select Web sites to include in their lessons or assignments. They could be used as a research and design tool to collect data about a particular Web site, or as guidelines for what features to include in a new Web site. In order to illustrate each of these uses, we decided to let some of the people who are actually using the instruments describe their innovative applications.

The *WebMAC* Instruments for Lesson Planning

In Chapter Eight, we focused on ways educators used the *WebMAC* instruments to teach student evaluation skills; the students *themselves* were the evaluators. They may also be used by educators as their own personal evaluation tools when making decisions about which Web sites are most appropriate for use in their instruction.

Our first lesson-planning gem comes from a library media specialist who used *WebMAC Middle* to help her select the Web sites she will recommend to her colleagues.

Gail Gilland is the library media specialist at Damascus (Virginia) Middle School and is also pursuing her master's degree in instructional technology at Virginia Polytechnical Institute. The program she is taking at Virginia Tech will culminate with her developing a personal "electronic portfolio" on the Web. We asked Gail what her portfolio would contain. "It will have my resume. It will have educational links that I am recommending, which can be in any categories that I come up with. My professional presentations that I do throughout the course will be posted on the Web, all under the umbrella of this portfolio. I will even include software evaluations," she explained.

As Gail mentioned, part of her portfolio will include educational links that she basically is endorsing. As a professional, visitors to her Web page would expect expert recommendations. That puts pressure on Gail to use her personal judgment about which Web sites would be most appropriate or valuable to her colleagues. This makes evaluation especially important to her. "Every time I get on the Web now, whether I am here at school or at home doing homework for my portfolio, I am constantly in the 'evaluate' mode," she said. So Gail uses the instrument as checklist to make decisions about which sites to include as links in her portfolio.

Gail also finds the instrument useful for helping her in a presentation course she is taking at Virginia Tech. "Right now, we are doing presentations every two to three days—electronic presentations on different things—so I'm having to go to a lot of Web sites to pick up information. Time is of the essence... and I find this instrument allows me to quickly go through the site."

Jennifer Skilton, who participated in the pilot study described in Chapter Three, said she first learned about *WebMAC Junior* at one of the librarian meetings in her school district. She said that finding Web sites that are "top level" has become an issue that her colleagues have been discussing. "It is something that we know our principals and administrators are interested in, finding the Web sites that are most valuable for the kids and that are going to work best with their research," she said. They are still in the beginning stages of putting a plan together toward that end. The *WebMAC* instruments could serve as tools that could be a part of a plan in which practitioners work together to identify top-level sites that can be used in classrooms.

 **The authors are using the *WebMAC* instruments as guidelines for the ongoing design of their motivation Web site (www.MotivationMining.com)**

The WebMAC Instruments for Research & Design

The *WebMAC* instruments are also useful as tools in research projects to analyze user responses and perceptions about a Web site in order to make recommendations for modification or revision, or as a checklist when designing an original site.

Our first gem in this category comes from the authors of this book. We used an earlier *WebMAC Junior* as part of a comprehensive formative research effort for a popular children's television program which aired nationally on The Learning Channel for three years, as of the publication date of this book. Formative research is intended to inform the production team and other decision-makers of what's working and what needs to be revised or tossed. It is called "formative" because it takes place while the program is still in the production phase; this way, changes can be made before it is publicly aired. Research after the fact is called "summative" research and looks at the overall results in terms of its stated objectives at the inception of the project.

The program called *Pappyland* was designed to encourage art and creativity in five- to nine-year-olds. We conducted research not only on the effects of the television program itself, but also on the motivational quality of its related Web site. Most television programs today have associated Web sites. You can generally see them "plugged" at the end of the television program itself. That is one way of getting first-time visitors. Keeping visitors once at the Web site and encouraging return visitors, however, depends on much more.

We used a multifaceted approach in our research. Data was collected from observations, focus groups, and the actual information that children provided through their *WebMAC* evaluations. We also collected information from educators and parents. When we were finished, we were able to pinpoint the strengths and provide recommendations on what could be done to improve the Web site in a number of areas. According to one of the members of our research team, Jean Van Doren, library media specialist at H.W. Smith Elementary School in Syracuse, New York, the biggest gripe kids had was the loading time for games. On the other hand, once they were able to access the games, it was one of their favorite things about the site.

If you are planning to use one of the *WebMAC* instruments as part of a research or evaluation project, we suggest that you also include at least one or two other methods for ensuring the richness of the information you collect. For example, following up the administration of the instrument with a focus group of children a day or so later allows you to probe for more detailed responses based on what you discovered in the instruments.

 As technology continues to evolve, more and more research will be conducted to explore learning in new environments. John Chadwick, Ed.D., is Senior Research Associate at the Institute for Learning Innovation, a private nonprofit organization in Annapolis, Maryland, that conducts research and evaluation in free-choice learning environments. The Institute and the New York Hall of Science are seeking funding for research on how the public uses science education Web sites. They want to know who uses these sites and for what purposes. John plans to use *WebMAC Middle* (and *WebMAC Senior*) to collect data. John told us, "As you can see, the *WebMAC* instruments will be invaluable for allowing us to assess whether the Web site even holds the attention of the online learner."

 This gem is mostly about *WebMAC Junior's* oldest sibling, *WebMAC Senior*, but there is promise in the future for "Junior" so here goes. Anise Ferreira, Ph.D., and Heloisa Collins, Ph.D, researchers at the Catholic University of Sao Paulo, Brazil, are exploring online language learning, course and material design and evaluation, and the effects of interface on learning. They are part of a larger research team that is investigating the interface between Distance Education and Applied Linguistics.

The team developed an online, Web-based course as part of the graduate program in applied linguistics and the Cultura Inglesa (British English school supported by the British Council). The purpose of the course was to improve the writing and oral performance of teachers of English working in state high schools in Sao Paulo. Anise used *WebMAC Senior* to evaluate similar courses. Now they will use the instrument to evaluate the motivational aspects of the Web-based instruction with about 70 adult Brazilian students enrolled in the online courses (English for Internet Users). Anise translated both *WebMAC Senior* and *WebMAC Junior* into Portuguese. She translated *WebMAC Junior* because she hopes to use it in a future course with elementary teachers. They'll develop two more courses offered to about 30 school teachers of English from several small rural towns. They'll use the *WebMAC* instrument as one data collection instrument. "*WebMAC* will give us a very important picture of part of this complex thing called learning on the Internet," Heloisa predicted.

Here's a nugget suggested by one of the reviewers of this book...

Locate some good and bad examples of Web sites. Have students compare them and then evaluate using *WebMAC Junior* to ensure competence.

The items on the WebMAC instruments can also be used as guidelines for the design of new Web sites. In this way, the instrument truly serves as a checklist for designers.

Earlier in this chapter, we described how Gail Gilland used *WebMAC Middle* as a way of evaluating the Web sites that she may include as links in her electronic portfolio. Well, Gail also is using *WebMAC Middle* for designing and modifying the school Web site at Damascus (Virginia) Middle School where she is the webmaster. Gail is able to use *WebMAC Middle* from an adult perspective, while constantly trying to maintain the eyes of a child, something her years of experience gives her the ability to do. She thinks *WebMAC Middle* is especially well-suited for middle-school-aged children. She explained, "I found (the items) very clear and concise. I think [with] some of the other models that I've seen, because they're written by adults, sometimes I almost felt like it was meant for adults' eyes only, and yet they were saying this is an activity that you can do with your students. And I didn't feel like it was. In fact, it was way over their heads." An important feature of the *WebMAC* instruments is that they were designed for and tested by kids.

When Gail first started designing the Web site two years ago, she admits she put "all these little animations and doodads in all over the place." However, that soon changed. "Once I started reviewing evaluation instruments like yours, and knowing what makes a good web page and what doesn't, and really defining yourself what you want your page to be, it's different..." she said.

Now Gail asks herself questions like "Do I want this page to be strictly a showcase for my school with lots of pictures of kids and things that will take forever to download? Or do I want it to be more of a jumping off point for my teachers and students so they can use their school's Web page as their own home page?" She wants *teachers* to be able to go to the school's page and be able to access sites that can be immediately helpful to them in the classroom. She also wants *students* to be able to access their school page from home and know that she, personally, has put some sites on the page that they can use for reports. Gail said, "I want to be very picky about the pages that I put on their [school Web site]—[so] that they are authoritative [and] designed well, but will not take forever to download and will be of help to students and teachers."

NUGGET

If your students are designing their own Web sites, remind them that it is fun to play around with all the possibilities technically, but that in the end, too much glitz and not enough substance will mean that visitors may not return.

COMING UP...

In Chapter Ten, we offer some final thoughts on the importance of evaluation skills for the information literate citizen of the 21st century.

HIGHLIGHTS of Chapter Nine

The *WebMAC* instruments have many uses. They can be used for planning lessons, aiding in the decision making process that determines which Web sites to use in classroom presentations and homework assignments. They also can be used in research to evaluate and compare existing Web sites. Finally, they can be used as a design tool for creating effective new Web sites.

 **MINESTORMING**

After reading Chapter Nine you probably have some ideas about some other ways to use *WebMAC Junior–2000* and *WebMAC Middle* that no one else has thought of. Make sure to record them below.

_____
_____
_____
_____
_____
_____
_____
_____
_____
_____

CHAPTER 10

Motivation Mining into the Future

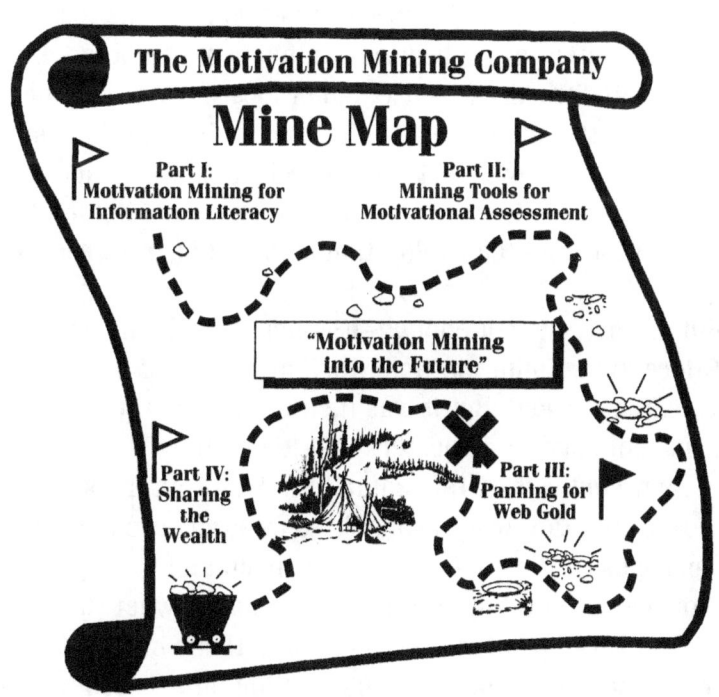

Introduction

All one needs to do is pay close attention to recent commercials on television to realize how much our world has changed. Ads for technology applications, hardware, software, and electronic services flood the airwaves. And almost every ad ends with a Web site address—just one more indication that the children of the new millennium must not only be comfortable with using technology, but must also be wise consumers of technology. This requires new skills and new tools.

Chapter Objectives

By the end of Chapter ten, you will:
▶ feel an "urge to action" to share with us your own creative ideas for helping students learn critical evaluation skills for the 21st century. (We hope!)

Information Skills for the 21st Century

Today's students are on the crest of a technology wave that is sweeping not only the country, but the world. The information literate citizen of the 21st century must possess the skills needed to effectively use technology and to add value to its potential applications. In his book *The Road Ahead*, Bill Gates looks back at the difficulty we once had of locating the best information for our needs and at the amount of time it took to find that information. He contrasts that with today's electronic search capabilities and our ability to look at information in different ways than we ever did before. "[This] flexibility invites exploration, and the exploration is invariably rewarded with discovery."[1]

But discovery is not enough—it is only part of the exploration process. In the 19th century, California Gold Rush miners used maps and word-of-mouth to search for gold. But it was their ability to "sift" and "differentiate" between real gold and its imposters that led them to the limited riches available. As we enter the 21st century, the Web continues to grow at an explosive rate, and the riches available to everyone are almost limitless. As new technologies emerge and evolve, the speed and quality of all forms of information and the level of interactivity available, what Gates calls "the global interactive network," provides access even to those in the most isolated parts of the world. The sheer amount of information on the Web makes using all of it impossible; the differences in quality among Web resources makes using all of it undesirable. The ability to evaluate and identify the highest quality Web resources becomes critical.

We have only just begun to uncover the treasures that lay beneath the surface of the Web and to refine the rich resources available for the taking. Successful information miners will possess the skills and tools to find the solutions to tomorrow's problems rather than spin their wheels still trying to figure out the questions.

Learning critical evaluation skills within a total information literacy program is essential for today's students to "thrive in an information rich future."[2] As educators, we must be sure that these skills and tools are within the grasp of all of our students to empower them to "stake their claim" and compete in the 21st century.

Final Thoughts

Throughout this book, we used a mining metaphor to provide a framework for evaluating the rich resources of the World Wide Web. We began by describing the importance of and relationships among information literacy, motivation, and the evaluation of Web resources. We then introduced some innovative Web evaluation instruments that focus on the motivational quality of Web sites while considering their content and functional capabilities. These "mining tools" were designed for students but may also be used by teachers, library media specialists, and others concerned with identifying the best resources for teaching and learning. We followed this with descriptions of a variety of practical applications for these tools, most of which came from K-12 educators, college instructors, and researchers.

We hope that the readers of this book will come away with a host of ideas that they can implement to meet their needs and the needs of their students. We invite readers to submit their Web evaluation success stories to us at our Web site (www.MotivationMining.com) so that they may be shared with the larger education community.

In Chapter Eleven, we provide all of the materials needed for an inservice workshop on Web evaluation for educators.

[1] B. Gates, *The Road Ahead*. New York, NY: Penguin Books, (Rev. ed.), 1996, pp. 135-6.

[2] M.B. Eisenberg and D. Johnson. "Computer Skills for Information Problem-Solving: Learning and Teaching Technology in Context." *ERIC Digest*. Clearinghouse on Information & Technology, March 1996, p. 4. (EDO-IR-96-04)

In order to be productive and contributing citizens of the 21st century, today's students must not only learn the *skills* necessary to be truly information literate, but they must also be capable of adding value to present technology applications. Furthermore, they must be able to think of new and creative ways to use the vast amount of information that is available to them.

Educators and students must possess essential evaluation skills and use effective evaluation *tools* to identify the highest quality Web resources for teaching and learning.

MINESTORMING

Although Chapter Ten was brief, it may have stirred some thoughts that you will want to preserve. Use this page to jot them down.

_____
_____
_____
_____
_____
_____
_____
_____
_____
_____

stage for the need for students to develop critical evaluation skills in order to identify and evaluate the highest quality Web sites available. Evaluation skills are essential to the information literate student. They will also be necessary to successfully compete and contribute in the information-rich 21st century. You might want to do the introduction informally and without overheads (other than the title overhead, which can stay on-screen), asking questions of the audience to get them in a participatory mood (e.g., "Does anyone know how often information doubles?"). Make sure you have the *latest* statistics. After warming up your audience, use your overheads to reinforce the main points using this content outline as a basic guide.

2. Next, define the term *Motivation Mining*: the identification and extraction of Web resources that have the potential of engaging students in the learning process by meeting important motivational criteria. This requires "sifting" through many Web sites to find the "gems." Motivation Mining is the responsibility of the educator.

3. The principles of Motivation Mining and the Web evaluation instrument are based on a well-known motivation theory, Expectancy-Value (or E-V) Theory. E-V theory states that there are two prerequisites for a person to be motivated to complete a task.

4. The first prerequisite is that the person must *value* the task. The second prerequisite is that the person must *expect to succeed* at the task. This is especially important for young children. If a child does not feel that he or she can be successful at a task, it is likely that the child will either withdraw from the activity or put forth only a minimal effort.

5. There are two important factors to consider when evaluating Web resources for teaching and learning. The first is CONTENT VALIDITY. When considering content, we must decide whether it is *appropriate* for the specific teaching need (e.g., on the appropriate learning level, curriculum-related, accurate, current, unbiased) and whether the content is *authentic*, that is, the source of the site is authoritative for the topic. But content validity is not enough when evaluating Web resources. [You can also refer to the *Content Validity Checklist* in Appendix A when discussing content validity and use it as a handout if you wish.]

6. The second essential factor is MOTIVATIONAL QUALITY; that is, the potential of the selected Web site to motivate students to learn. If a Web site is high in Motivational Quality, students will want to remain at the Web site to explore it and will revisit it for future learning.

7. If you think back to E-V Theory, Motivational Quality has two dimensions: **Value** and **Expectation for Success**. For Web sites, "Value" means providing information and activities that students perceive as valuable and personally relevant. "Expectation for Success" means providing an environment in which students feel confident that they can be successful

in navigating and using the Web site. At this point, you might want to ask your workshop participants a question or two (e.g., "What kinds of things do you think would help create a Web site environment that encourages a high expectation for success in young students?"). If they don't come up with anything, tell them that they will find out in just a moment or two (i.e., Overhead #9). Or give them a clue or two. You might also want to mention, here, that when discussing Value with children, we use the term "how interesting" and when discussing Expectation for Success, we use the phrase "how well it works."

8. The two factors of Motivational Quality are multiplicative. Both must be present for the Web site to be highly motivating.

9. Motivational Quality is defined in terms of four attributes. Two attributes, "Stimulating" and "Meaningful," relate to Value, while "Organized" and "Easy-to-Use" describe Expectation for Success.

10. For a Web site to be "Stimulating," it must contain features that capture and maintain interest and stimulate curiosity. A "Meaningful" Web site has elements that add personal value and promote relevance. (Try brainstorming ideas for adding Value, if you have time.)

11. An "Organized" Web site has features that provide a logical overall structure and sequence to facilitate understanding of the Web site's content. A Web site is "Easy-to-Use" when it includes various navigation aids and help mechanisms.

12. What makes the Web evaluation instrument different than others you might know? Two things: (1) It has a theoretical base (E-V Theory), and (2) it focuses on *motivational* issues. Although it focuses on motivational issues, it covers many issues that children should consider when evaluating Web sites in general. Thus, it is widely used as a general evaluation instrument for children.

13. The *Web Site Motivational Analysis Checklist* (*WebMAC*, for short) is available at several student levels: *WebMAC Junior–2000* for grades 1-4; *WebMAC Middle* for grades 5-8; and *WebMAC Senior* for grade 9 and up. [If you wish, you could also mention *Web Site Investigator*, a very brief questionnaire without scoring grids.] Today, we will focus on *WebMAC Junior–2000*. These instruments have been widely tested and validated. As you will soon see, they provide a set of grids for visually representing scores.

14. *WebMAC Junior–2000* can be used in three ways. It can be used to teach students important evaluation skills as part of an information literacy program. It can be used as a lesson-planning tool for identifying the best Web resources to incorporate into lessons or students' homework assignments. It can also be used as a research and design tool to compare Web sites or provide guidance for design of a new Web site.

15. *[This overhead can serve as an organizing framework for the next activities as follows: Select a Web site that participants can evaluate during the workshop. Pass out copies of the instrument and go through directions. Give them sufficient time to complete the instrument (approximately 45 minutes). When they have finished, have them reconvene, and review the scoring mechanisms. Then, debrief them on results.]*
16. *[Have participants brainstorm ways they could use WebMAC Junior-2000 with their students in their subject areas.]*

NOTE: Mention that for the upper elementary grades, the *WebMAC Middle* instrument might be useful because of its more sophisticated appearance and additional items. The theoretical framework is exactly the same as what was covered in the workshop; the scoring differences are explained in the administration directions. It is your decision whether you choose to provide the *WebMAC Middle* instrument as part of your workshop.

Overhead Transparency Masters

On the next 16 pages you will find a set of reproducible overhead transparency masters which you may use in a workshop on Web site evaluation for your colleagues.

Motivation Mining the Web

Inservice Workshop for Elementary Educators

1

What is Motivation Mining?

"Motivation Mining"

is the identification and extraction of Web resources that have the potential of engaging students in the learning process by meeting important motivational criteria.

*As in mining in the traditional sense, one must "**sift**" through many Web sites in search of the "gems."*

Theory

The principles of *Motivation Mining* are grounded primarily in Expectancy-Value Theory (E-V)

E-V Theory states that there are two prerequisites for a person to be motivated to complete a task.

E-V Theory

The person must VALUE the task.

The person must have an EXPECTATION FOR SUCCESS at the task.

Two Important Factors in Evaluating Web Sites...

Content Validity

Appropriateness for teaching need (e.g., appropriate learning level, curriculum-related, accurate, current, unbiased, etc.)

Authenticity (credible site author or owner)

As educator, YOU are the judge!

BUT... Content Validity is a necessary but *insufficient* condition for a successful teaching episode!

Two Important Factors in Evaluating Web Sites...

Motivational Quality

Determines the potential of the selected Web site to motivate students to learn.

If the motivational quality is high, students:

▼ Will want to remain at Web site and explore.

▼ May wish to revisit the Web site at another time for future learning experiences.

Motivational Quality of Web Sites

Value
The Web site should provide information and activities that students perceive as valuable and personally relevant.

Expectation for Success
The Web site should provide an environment in which students feel confident that they can be successful in navigating and using the Web site.

Motivational Quality of Web Sites

Multiplicative Function:

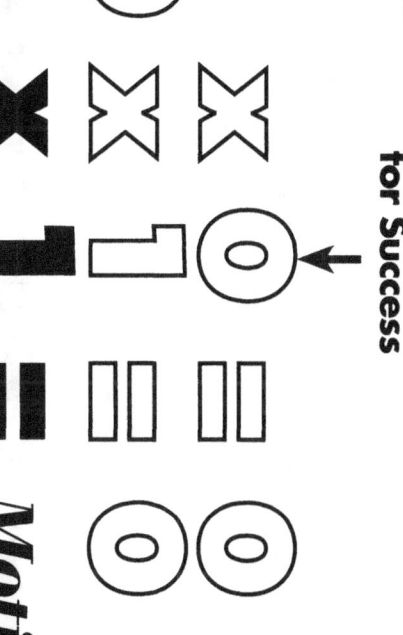

Motivating!

The number "1" refers to the presence of a factor, while "0" refers to the absence of a factor.

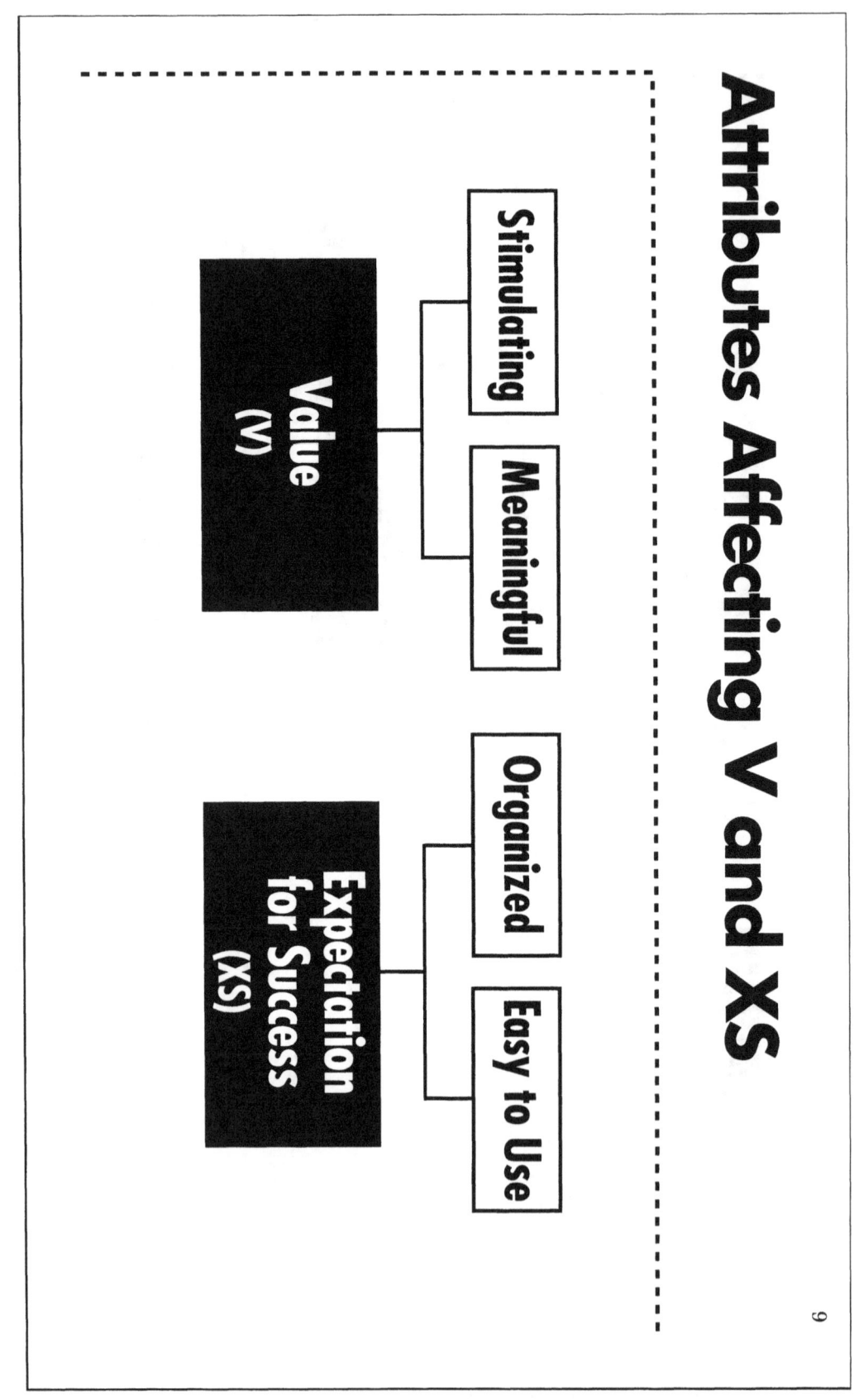

Value

Stimulating: *has features that*
- ▼ capture and maintain interest
- ▼ stimulate curiosity

Meaningful: *includes elements that*
- ▼ add personal value
- ▼ promote relevance

Expectation for Success

Organized: *has features that*
- ▼ provide a logical overall structure
- ▼ facilitate understanding of the Web site's content

Easy-to-Use: *includes elements such as*
- ▼ navigational aids
- ▼ help mechanisms
- ▼ links that work

Motivational Assessment

There are many Web evaluation tools.

Few have a theoretical base.

Most focus on content or functionality (functionality refers to how well the technical aspects of the site work).

Few address motivational issues.

The *WebMAC* instruments consider all factors framed in terms of their effect on student motivation.

Motivational Assessment

Web Site Motivational Analysis Checklist (WebMAC)

▼ set of three instruments for use of students
  ▽ WebMAC Junior–2000 for grades 1-4
  ▽ WebMAC Middle for grades 5-8
  ▽ WebMAC Senior for grades 9 and up
▼ based on E-V theory
▼ tested and validated
▼ provides set of grids for visually representing scores

Motivational Assessment

WebMAC Junior–2000 can be used:

▼ To help teach students evaluation skills, an important aspect of information literacy.

▼ As a lesson-planning tool when you are evaluating a Web site for use in any curricular unit.

▼ As a research and design tool for practitioners conducting their own research on motivational effectiveness of Web sites or designing a new Web site.

Using WebMAC Junior—2000 to Mine Web "Gems"

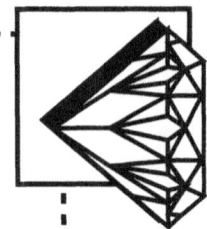

- ▼ The Directions
- ▽ Administration
- ▽ Scoring
- ▼ The instrument
- ▼ Practice
- ▼ Debrief

"MINE" STORMING

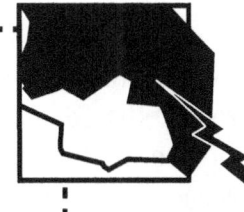

Let's think of some ideas for using *WebMAC Junior–2000* with students.

Handouts

On the next three pages you will find the reproducible handout masters for the participants in your workshop for educators. You could also reproduce the *Content Validity Checklist* in Appendix A as a handout. You might also want to consider providing your participants with a packet of overheads geared toward younger learners, which they can use to introduce *WebMAC Junior–2000* to their students. These can be found in Chapter Twelve.

Certificate of Achievement

Following the handout pages, you will find a Certificate of Achievement which you can copy and give to participants at the conclusion of the "Motivation Mining the Web" workshop, if you choose.

Motivation Mining the Web

Inservice Workshop for Elementary Educators

What is Motivation Mining?

"**Motivation Mining**" is the identification and extraction of Web resources that have the potential of engaging students in the learning process by meeting important motivational criteria.

As in mining in the traditional sense, one must "sift" through many Web sites in search of the "gems."

Theory

The principles of *Motivation Mining* are grounded primarily in Expectancy-Value Theory (E-V)

E-V Theory states that there are two prerequisites for a person to be motivated to complete a task.

E-V Theory

The person must VALUE the task.

The person must have an EXPECTATION FOR SUCCESS at the task.

Two Important Factors in Evaluating Web Sites...

Content Validity

Appropriateness for teaching need (e.g., appropriate learning level, curriculum-related, accurate, current, unbiased, etc.)

Authenticity (credible site author or owner)

As educator, YOU are the judge!

BUT... Content Validity is a necessary but ***insufficient*** condition for a successful teaching episode!

Two Important Factors in Evaluating Web Sites...

Motivational Quality

Determines the potential of the selected Web site to motivate students to learn.

If the motivational quality is high, students:

▶ Will want to remain at Web site and explore.

▶ May wish to revisit the Web site at another time for future learning experiences.

Motivational Quality of Web Sites

Value
The Web site should provide information and activities that students perceive as valuable and personally relevant.

Expectation for Success
The Web site should provide an environment in which students feel confident that they can be successful in navigating and using the Web site.

Motivational Quality of Web Sites

Multiplicative Function:

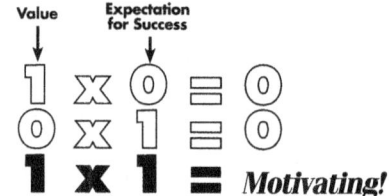

$1 \times 1 =$ *Motivating!*

The number "1" refers to the presence of a factor, while "0" refers to the absence of a factor.

Attributes Affecting V and XS

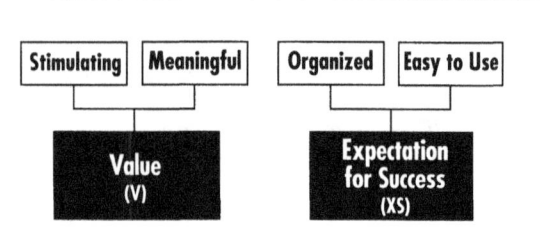

Value

Stimulating: *has features that*
- ▶ capture and maintain interest
- ▶ stimulate curiosity

Meaningful: *includes elements that*
- ▶ add personal value
- ▶ promote relevance

Expectation for Success

Organized: *has features that*
- ▶ provide a logical overall structure
- ▶ facilitate understanding of the Web site's content

Easy-to-Use: *includes elements such as*
- ▶ navigational aids
- ▶ help mechanisms
- ▶ links that work

Motivational Assessment

There are many Web evaluation tools.

Few have a theoretical base.

Most focus on content or functionality (functionality refers to how well the technical aspects of the site work).

Few address motivational issues.

The *WebMAC* instruments consider all factors framed in terms of their effect on student motivation.

Motivational Assessment

Web Site Motivational Analysis Checklist (WebMAC)
- ▶ set of three instruments for use of students
  - ▷ *WebMAC Junior–2000* for grades 1-4
  - ▷ *WebMAC Middle* for grades 5-8
  - ▷ *WebMAC Senior* for grades 9 and up
- ▶ based on E-V theory
- ▶ tested and validated
- ▶ provides set of grids for visually representing scores

Motivational Assessment

***WebMAC Junior–2000* can be used:**
- ▶ To help teach students evaluation skills, an important aspect of information literacy.
- ▶ As a lesson-planning tool when you are evaluating a Web site for use in any curricular unit.
- ▶ As a research and design tool for practitioners conducting their own research on motivational effectiveness of Web sites or designing a new Web site.

Using *WebMAC Junior—2000* to Mine Web "Gems"

- ▶ The Directions
  - ▷ Administration
  - ▷ Scoring
- ▶ The instrument
- ▶ Practice
- ▶ Debrief

"MINE"STORMING

Let's think of some ideas for using
WebMAC Junior–2000
with students.

Certificate of Achievement

Motivation Mining the Web

Inservice Workshop for Elementary Educators

Presented By

Name

Date

 **COMING UP...**

In Chapter Twelve, you will find some materials that you can use in the classroom or library media center when providing background information to your students on *WebMAC Junior–2000*.

 **HIGHLIGHTS of Chapter Eleven**

In Chapter Eleven, you received everything you will need to provide a workshop for your colleagues on motivation mining the Web. This included a workshop outline, overhead transparencies, and handouts. To reinforce the importance of teaching critical evaluation skills to their students, use current statistics about Web usage and growth. Whenever possible, get your audience in a participatory mood by asking questions and getting them involved. Finally, add something of yourself to the workshop. Make it your own. Minestorm some ideas for this on the next page!

 **MINESTORMING**

Do you have any ideas you might want to incorporate into your workshop? They could be strategies you think of to maintain participants' interest and build relevance; or perhaps, an activity you would like to include. Take a moment and minestorm any such ideas while they are fresh in your mind.

_____
_____
_____
_____
_____
_____
_____
_____
_____
_____

CHAPTER 12

Teaching Students to Use *WebMAC Junior–2000*

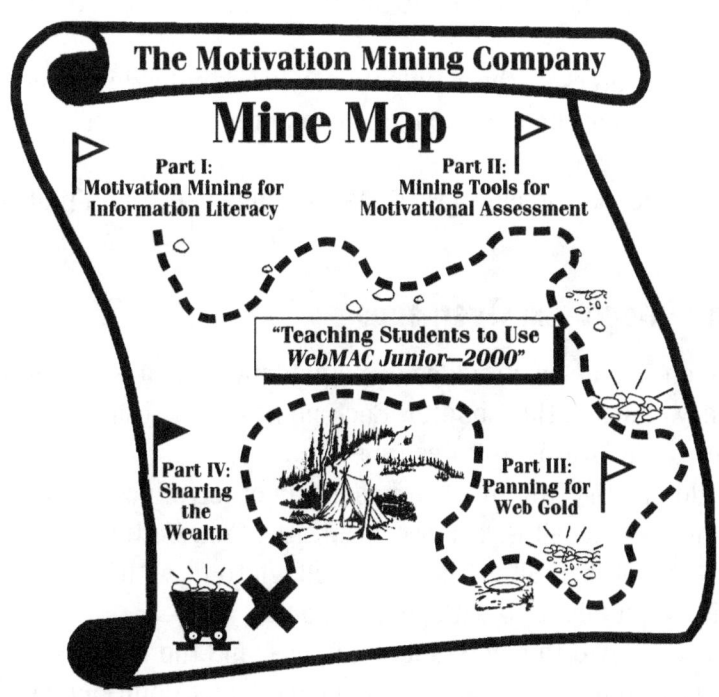

Introduction

In talking to educators about the *WebMAC* instruments, we found that some of them were taking the time to make overhead transparencies to help students before they actually filled out the instruments. This was over and above the actual lesson plan they created on evaluation. We thought that in Chapter Twelve, we would provide some overhead masters that might be useful and save you time, as well. In no way, are we suggesting an actual lesson plan like those you read about in Chapter Eight. We did not want to be restrictive in terms of our readers' creativity in designing their own plans. Instead, we offer these overhead masters so that you might integrate them into whatever lesson or unit on evaluation you create.

Chapter Objectives

After completing Chapter Twelve, you will be able to:
▶ incorporate the overhead transparency masters into a lesson plan of your own design on teaching children skills for evaluating Web sites.

Materials

Before introducing W*ebMAC Junior–2000* (or *WebMAC Middle*), you will need:
▶ Enough computers so that students may work individually or in pairs. Or, if working in a group situation, one computer wired to the Internet and a projection system.
▶ Copies of the instrument, directions, scoring sheets, and plotting grids.

Outline for Integrating Overheads

The outline below provides some guidance for presenting the overhead transparency slides in this chapter. Each point in the outline below references the number of the overhead it describes.

1. You could use the first overhead as a way of introducing the concept of evaluation of Web sites. The overhead title, "You Be the Judge: Taking a Closer Look at Web Sites," is broad enough to fit with many possible directions you might go with your lesson.
2. Use this overhead to help students understand the importance of learning to evaluate Web resources, revealing each bullet point one by one to reduce visual overload. The first bullet point can be used to discuss how

big the World Wide Web has grown. The second and third bullets can be part of an interactive dialog on what makes good and bad sites. You can stress the importance of accurate (believable or true) information, and up-to-date information. How do you know the answers to these questions? Are there any clues on a Web site? (e.g., a date the Web site was last revised, information on the author) You can also talk about how well a Web site works and what things to look for (e.g., loading time of graphics, ease to finding what you need)

3. Use this overhead for a quick discussion of key terms students should understand before using a Web assessment instrument. Young students will need help understanding what it means to "evaluate" a Web site. "You be the judge" of what is good or bad about a Web site is one way to start. Young children may also need explanation of what "information" is, and that it is broader than just facts or words.

4. Use this overhead to introduce *WebMAC Junior–2000*. Stress that it is not a test and there are no wrong answers. Point out that the instrument measures the quality of a Web site.

5. You can use this overhead to talk specifically about the kind of things the questionnaire measures.

6. Overheads #6–#10 are the *WebMAC Junior–2000* questions reproduced in a size that will be readable when projected in a classroom or LMC. Use the directions included with the instrument to explain the smiley faces and rating system. Overhead #6 includes the first four questions. Question #3 refers to the authenticity of the site. This question could be used to prompt a discussion on how one might decide if the information is credible (based on factors such as the author's background, organization, research support)

7. This overhead includes questions #5–#8. Question # 6 (Was it easy to find what you needed at this Web site?) is deliberately general. It can refer to information if students are engaged in a research project or homework assignment. That information could be in the form of text, graphics, sound, animation, or another format. For students who may be visiting a site for interest value as opposed to research, "what you needed" could refer to what they hoped to find at the Web site. The main word to focus on, however, is "easy," since it refers to how well the site works. If it was not easy to find what a student needed, the site may have poor navigational aids or other organizational problems.

8. This overhead includes questions #9–#12. Question #11 (Do you think this Web site sometimes adds new things to read about and do?) refers to how current the Web site is. This question could prompt a discussion of the clues students can look for at a site that would give them an idea of how up-to-date the site is (e.g., a date on the site that tells when it was last

revised; a flashing icon that reads "Coming Next Month. . .").

9. Overhead #9 includes Questions #13–#16. Question #14 is again deliberately general in its wording. This is so that it can apply to information, graphics, music, video, and topics of interest to the student.

10. Overhead #10 includes the two open-ended questions at the end of the questionnaire. If you are using *WebMAC Junior–2000* as a group activity, you could solicit responses from your students and write them on the overhead. What some students liked, others may not. This is a good time to reinforce that everyone is expected to have their own opinions when doing an evaluation.

11. You can use Overhead #11 to demonstrate to students how to score their instruments individually. Remind them that the numbers go across rather than up and down.

12. Once students have scored their own instruments, you can use Overhead #12 to demonstrate how to plot their scores. You might wish to take a student's score sheet to show a real example. Show them how to draw lines from each score to the intersection point. Then, describe what it means to be in each quadrant (refer to Chapter Seven for interpretation). You might even wish to write this information on the overhead itself as you are explaining, as one teacher we know did. You can reproduce this overhead twice if you also wish to grid the class average scores.

13. Overhead #13 is an overlay to Overhead #12. Once students grasp how to plot their scores, you can add this overlay to demonstrate where really good Web sites fall. You may wish to tape these transparencies together a head of time so that they align correctly.

14. Overhead #14 is the Class Tally. Use this if you decide to average all the students' scores on a particular Web site. You can have each student call out his or her scores for A and B as you place them on the overhead. One LMS told us she used a calculator to quickly tally up and average the scores. Then, she plotted the average scores on the grid for the class to see and discussed the results.

Overhead Transparency Masters

On the following 14 pages you will find the reproducible overhead transparency masters to be used with the outline above.

You Be the Judge!

Taking a Closer Look at Web Sites!

WWW Motivation Mining: Finding Treasures for Teaching Evaluation Skills, Grades 1-6 — Chapter 12: Teaching Students to Use *WebMAC Junior—2000*

Why Take a Closer Look?

- There are lots and lots of Web sites on every topic you can imagine.

- How do you know you have found the best Web site(s) for your homework or for your research projects? Or even just for what interests you?

- You must learn how to evaluate Web sites (that means decide for yourself how interesting, useful, and believable a site is, and how well it works.)

What Do These Words Mean?

HOME PAGE

BUTTON

LINK

Information

EVALUATE

Evaluating Web Sites

WebMAC Junior – 2000

- lets YOU be the judge!
- measures the quality of a Web site
- <u>no</u> <u>wrong</u> answers

WebMAC Junior – 2000

Helps You Decide:

1. How interesting and useful a Web site is to you

   and

2. How well the Web site works

Let's take a look at some of the WebMAC questions...

#5

CHAPTER 12: TEACHING STUDENTS TO USE *WebMAC Junior—2000*

WebMAC Junior – 2000

Web Site Address: _____

1. Was this an interesting or fun Web site to explore?

   0   1   2   3

2. Could you read and understand most of the words that were used?

   0   1   2   3

3. Was the information on this Web site believable? (Did it seem to be true?)

   0   1   2   3

4. Was it easy to find your way around without getting lost?

   0   1   2   3

#6

5. Did the pictures, sounds, or videos make this Web site more interesting?

☹ 😐 🙂 😃
0   1   2   3

6. Was it easy to find what you needed at this Web site?

☹ 😐 🙂 😃
0   1   2   3

7. Did this Web site have links to other interesting or useful Web sites?

☹ 😐 🙂 😃
0   1   2   3

8. Did all the parts of the Web site work the way they should?

☹ 😐 🙂 😃
0   1   2   3

#7

#8

9. Were there lots of activities to do on this Web site?

  ☺
0   1   2   3

10. Were the directions for using this Web site simple and clear?

  ☺
0   1   2   3

11. Do you think this Web site sometimes adds new things to read about and do?

☹  ☺ ☺
0   1   2   3

12. Did things like pictures, games, or videos *quickly* come up on the screen?

☹   ☺
0   1   2   3

#9

13. Did you like the colors and backgrounds used at this Web site?

　　　☹　　😐　　🙂　　😊
　　　0　　 1　　 2　　 3

14. Did you find *enough* of what you were looking for at this Web site?

　　　☹　　😐　　🙂　　😊
　　　0　　 1　　 2　　 3

15. Was what you found at this Web site useful to you?

　　　☹　　😐　　🙂　　😊
　　　0　　 1　　 2　　 3

16. Were there ways of getting help if you needed it at this Web site?

　　　☹　　😐　　🙂　　😊
　　　0　　 1　　 2　　 3

#10

Would you like to visit this Web site again sometime? (✓) YES ☐ NO ☐

Is this a Web site that friends your age would like to visit? YES ☐ NO ☐

⇩ What did you like **best** about this Web site? Write in the space below.

⇩ What would you do to make this Web site **better**? Write your ideas below.

✋ STOP

Scoring WebMAC Junior - 2000

#11

A		**B**
1. ___		2. ___
3. ___		4. ___
5. ___		6. ___
7. ___		8. ___
9. ___		10. ___
11. ___		12. ___
13. ___		14. ___
15. ___		16. ___
TOTAL A: ___		TOTAL B: ___

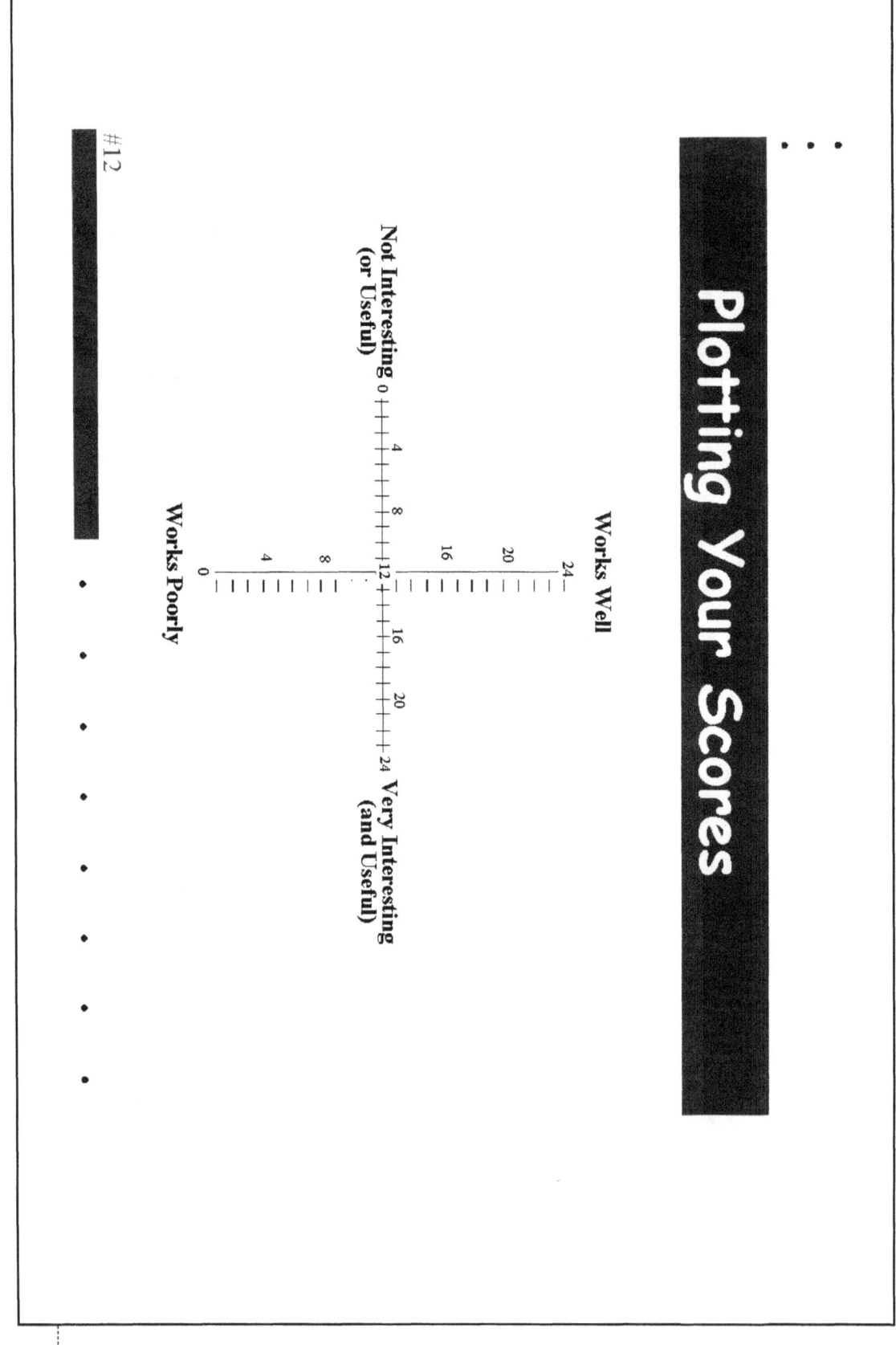

#13

Awesome
Website!

Good for both
interesting &
works well

Average for both
interesting &
works well

Class Tally

Individual Total A Scores

1. ____
2. ____
3. ____
4. ____
5. ____
6. ____
7. ____
8. ____
9. ____
10. ____
11. ____
12. ____
13. ____
14. ____
15. ____
16. ____
17. ____
18. ____
19. ____
20. ____

TOTAL A SCORES: ____
AVERAGE A SCORES: ____

Individual Total B Scores

1. ____
2. ____
3. ____
4. ____
5. ____
6. ____
7. ____
8. ____
9. ____
10. ____
11. ____
12. ____
13. ____
14. ____
15. ____
16. ____
17. ____
18. ____
19. ____
20. ____

TOTAL B SCORES: ____
AVERAGE B SCORES: ____

#14

The *AWA*rd Nomination Form

In Chapter Eight, we invited entire classes of students to nominate their favorite curriculum-related Web sites for the *AWA*rd or the Awesome Web site Award. Feel free to visit our Web site (www.MotivationMining.com) to download a nomination form.

 **COMING UP...**

Next up are the Appendices which include the *Content Validity Checklist* mentioned in Chapter Two, several complete lesson plans, and additional *WebMAC* instruments, tally sheets, and grids.

 **HIGHLIGHTS of Chapter Twelve**

In Chapter Twelve, you were provided with overhead transparency masters to use when introducing *WebMAC Junior–2000* or *WebMAC Middle*. Again, these materials were designed to be incorporated into your own lesson plan or unit on evaluation. You might get some ideas for possible lessons from Chapter Eight or from the Appendices. We also included overheads of the actual instrument for use when you review a Web site in a group situation.

 **MINESTORMING**

Take a moment to jot down any ideas you could incorporate when presenting *WebMAC Junior–2000* to your students.

_____
_____
_____
_____
_____
_____
_____
_____
_____
_____

Bibliography

Bibliography

Abel, F. J., and Abel J. P. (1996, October 18). *Integrating Mathematics and Social Studies: Activities Based on Internet Resources*. Paper presented at the Annual Meeting of the Montana Council of Teachers of Mathematics, Helena, MT. (Eric Document Reproduction Service No. ED401271).

Alexander, J., and Tate, M. (1998). "Teaching Web Evaluation: Meeting the Challenge." *Internet Trend Watch for Libraries, 3* (2). Librarians and Educators Online.

American Association of School Librarians and Association for Educational Communications and Technology (1998). *Information Power: Building Partnerships for Learning*. Chicago: American Library Association.

Arnone, M. P., and Small, R. V. (1999, March-April). "Evaluating the Motivational Effectiveness of Children's Web Sites." *Educational Technology, 39* (2).

Bloom, B. S., et. al (1971). *Handbook on Formative and Summative Evaluation of Student Learning*. New York: McGraw-Hill.

Boyer, C. L. (1996). "Using Museum Resources in the K-12 Social Studies Curriculum." *ERIC Digest*. Bloomington, IN: ERIC Clearinghouse for Social Studies/Social Science Education, (ED412174).

Brophy, J. (1998). *Motivating Students to Learn*. Boston: McGraw-Hill.

Burton, F.G., Chen, Y., Grover, V., and Stewart, K.A. (1992-3, Winter). "An Application of Expectancy Theory for Assessing User Motivation to Utilize an Expert System." *Journal of Management Information Systems, 9* (3).

Caywood, C. (1998). *Library Selection Criteria for WWW Resources*. <http://www.pilot.infi.net/~carolyn/criteria.html>.

Eisenberg, M. B. (1996, September.). "Take the Internet Challenge: Using Technology in Context." *The Book Report, V. 15* (Sept/Oct 96) p. supp 5-7. Special supplement.

Eisenberg, M. B., and Johnson, D. (1996, March). "Computer Skills for Information Problem-Solving: Learning and Teaching Technology in Context." *ERIC Digest*. ERIC Clearinghouse on Information & Technology. (EDO-IR-96-04).

Eisenberg, M. B., and Berkowitz, R. E. (1990). *Information Problem-solving: The Big Six Skills Approach to Library & Information Skills Instruction*. Norwood, NJ: Ablex Publishing Corporation.

Finder, K., and Raleigh, D. (1998, March 10-14). "Establishing a Framework Useful for Developing Web-Based Assignments in K-12 Education." In SITE 98: Society for Information Technology & Teacher Education International Conference, Washington, DC – Published in Proceedings. (ED421099).

Gates, B. (1996). *The Road Ahead* (Rev. ed.). New York: Penguin Books

Gilster, P. (1997). *Digital Literacy*. New York: Wiley.

Hackbarth, S. (1997). "Web-Based Learning in the Context of K-12 Schooling." In *Educational Media and Technology Yearbook*, Vol. 22.

Hansen, D. (1989). "Lesson Evading and Lesson Dissembling: Ego Strategies in the Classroom." *American Journal of Education*, Vol. 97.

International Society for Technology in Education (1998, June). *National Educational Technology Standards for Students*, NETS Project Report.

Keller, J. M. (1987). "Strategies for Stimulating the Motivation to Learn." *Performance and Instruction*, Vol. 26 (8).

Kuhlthau, C. (1993). "Implementing a Process Approach to Information Skills: A Study Identifying Indicators of Success in Library Media Programs." *School Library Media Quarterly*, Vol. 22 (1).

Kuhlthau, C. (1985). *Teaching the Library Research Process*. West Nyack, NY: The Center for Applied Research in Education.

Lankes, R. D., and Kasowitz, A. S. (1998). *AskA Starter Kit: How to Build and Maintain Digital Reference Services*. Syracuse, NY: ERIC Clearinghouse on Information & Technology.

Leu, D. J., Jr.; Leu, D. D.; and Leu, K. R. (1999). *Teaching with the Internet: Lessons from the Classroom*. Norwood, MA: Christopher-Gordon Publishers.

McKenzie, J. (1996). "Making WEB Meaning." *Educational Leadership*, Vol. 54 (3).

Mendels, P. (1998, April 28). "Study Shows Students Use Internet Primarily for Research." *The New York Times on the Web*. <http://www.nytimes.com/library/tech/98/04/cyber/articles/28education.html>.

Nielsen, J. (1994). "Heuristic Evaluation." In J. Nielsen and R.L. Mack (Eds.), *Usability Inspection Methods*. New York: John Wiley & Sons.

Pappas, M. L., and Tepe, A. E. (1995). "Follett Information Skills Model." In *Teaching Electronic Information Skills*. McHenry, IL: Follett Software Company.

"Public Schools with Internet Access Make Significant Strides in 1998." (1999, March 3). *Educational Technology News*, Vol.16 (5). Business Publishers, Inc.

Rademann, T. *Information Unlimited: Employing Internet Resources in Education* <http://www.isoc.org/inet97/proceedings/D3/D3_1.HTM>.

Schrock, K. (1998). "Evaluation of World Wide Web Sites: An Annotated Bibliography." ERIC Digest. (EDO-IR-98-02).

Seigel, B. (1997, October). "Eureka! Discovering Inventions and Technology." *Technology Connection*.

Small, R. V. (1997). "Assessing the Motivational Quality of World Wide Web sites." *ERIC Digest*, (ED407930).

Small, R. V., and Arnone, M. P. (1999). *Turning Kids on to Research: The Power of Motivation*. Englewood, CO: Libraries Unlimited.

Small, R. V., and Arnone, M. P. (1999, May/June). "Motivation Mining: Prospecting the Web." *The Book Report*, Vol. 18 (1).

Small, R. V., and Arnone, M. P. (1999, February). "Web Site Quality: Do Students Know It When They See It?" *School Library Media Activities Monthly*, XV (6).

Small, R., and Lee, B. (1999). "Web-Based Resources for K-12 Instructional Planning." In R. M. Branch and M. A. Fitzgerald (Eds.), *Educational Media and Technology Yearbook*, Vol. 24.

Snead, K. C., Jr., and Harrell, A. M. (1995). "An Application of Expectancy Theory to Explain a Manager's Intention to Use a Decision Support System." *Decision Sciences*, Vol. 25 (4).

Stripling, B. K., and Pitts, J. M. (1988). *Brainstorms and Blueprints*. Englewood, CO: Libraries Unlimited.

Tillman, M. (1998). *Education Metasites*. ERIC Clearinghouse on Information & Technology, (ED423877).

Tobiason, K. (1997, April). "Tailoring the Internet to Primary Classrooms." *Technology Connections*.

Wlodkowski, R. J. (1993). *Enhancing Adult Motivation to Learn: A Guide to Improving Instruction and Increasing Learner Achievement*. San Francisco: Jossey-Bass Publishers.

Vroom, V. H. (1995). *Work and Motivation*. San Franciso: Jossey-Bass.

Yucht, A. (1997). *FLIP IT! An Information Skills Strategy for Student Researchers*. Worthington, OH: Linworth Publishing, Inc.

Appendices

Appendix A:
Content Validity Checklist

CONTENT VALIDITY CHECKLIST (ARNONE & SMALL, 1999)

The Content Validity Checklist was designed as a Web-aid for teachers screening Web sites for inclusion in lesson plans. This checklist focuses on content validity only. There are no questions about functionality, amount of information, appeal of visuals, or navigation issues since these are included in the *WebMAC* instruments. For content validity to be high, all boxes should be checked "Yes," unless an item is not applicable to your situation.

1. The source of information for this Web site is credible. YES ☐ No ☐

   TIP **Check the home page to determine who or what entity is responsible for the content. Is there a link to background information on the author(s) or institution? Make sure you are convinced of the legitimacy and qualifications of the author.**

2. There is a way to contact the author of the Web site, if necessary. YES ☐ No ☐

3. The factual information or content of the Web site seems accurate. YES ☐ No ☐

   TIP **Look for the sources of information. They should be clearly identified and easily verifiable. Links to other Web sites with related information may also help with verification**

4. If the Web site presents concepts or principles in its domain (e.g., science, art), they are appropriately presented without confusing or missing information. YES ☐ No ☐

   TIP **Think of your target audience. Is there enough baseline information presented to support the presentation of higher order concepts or principles?**

5. There are no typographical or spelling errors that could potentially cause the information at this Web site to be misunderstood. YES ☐ No ☐

6. The content is appropriate for your students' developmental level? YES ☐ No ☐

7. The links from this site appear to be credible. YES ☐ No ☐

8. This Web site appears to be free of bias. YES ☐ No ☐

   TIP **Is there a reason the author of this Web site might be biased in the presentation of content? (For example, does the author have a vested interest in how you react**

to the information provided?) Does the author identify when a statement is a personal point of view?

9. The information on this Web site is current enough for your needs.   YES ☐   No ☐

> **TIP:** Look for a "Last Update" usually located at the header or footer of a page. Often, some parts of the site will be updated regularly, while others remain fairly constant. Determine how important currency is to the presentation of your specific topic.

10. The links from this Web site are also current and unbiased.   YES ☐   No ☐

Appendix B:
Lesson Plans

LESSON PLAN #1

Lake Street Elementary by Deb Christensen

Description:

The purpose of this lesson is to have students begin discussing the evaluation of resources. The students will practice by evaluating books and a Web site.

Objectives:

1. The students will be able to state two things they should look at when selecting a book.
2. The students will navigate a Web site.
3. The students will evaluate a non-fiction book and a Web site.

Duration:

Two 30-40 minute class periods.

Day 1:

Essential Resources:

World atlas
The following three books or similar titles:
Santa's New Suit by Mike Lester (Illustrator)
Squids Will be Squids: Fresh Morals, Beastly Fables by Jon Scieszka
Indian Sign Language by Robert Hofsinde
An assortment of nonfiction books
An evaluation form (attached)
Big6 Pizza Wheel

Directions:

1. Select four books—a large plain covered world atlas, a very small book that is a student favorite, a book with vivid illustrations that might not have a lot of information, and a book with simple line drawing illustrations that covers a topic the students would be interested in. Cover the front of the first small book so students cannot see the title and illustration. Cover the front of the last two books so the students can see the covers and part of the illustrations but not the titles. Examples: *Santa's New Suit*, *Squids Will be Squids*, and *Indian Sign Language*.
2. Hold up the first two books in front of the students and ask them which book they would select if they could check one of the books out today.

3. Ask the students the reason for their selection.
4. Show the students that the large book is a world atlas and that the small book is one of their favorite stories (*Santa's New Suit*).
5. Now hold up the other two books and ask the students which one they would select to check out and why.
6. Show the students that one book (*Squids Will be Squids*) has bold illustrations but it doesn't contain a lot of information. Show the students that the other book with a plain cover and simple line drawings *(Indian Sign Language)* has a lot of good information.
7. Talk to the students about how the cover of a book can be misleading. Discuss how to make good choices when selecting a book. Ask students what they should look at when selecting a book. Possible answers include vocabulary; is the reading level appropriate; author; facts; and so on.
8. Have the students select a non-fiction book from a pre-selected set of books. Give the students time to look at the book (about 10-20 minutes).
9. Hand out the evaluation form and go over the directions with the students.
10. Ask the students to use the form to evaluate the book they have been looking at.
11. After the students have completed the evaluation form, discuss with them the *Big6* pizza wheel and what kind of information they would be looking for in books.

Day 2:

Essential Resources:

Big6 Pizza Wheel
WebMAC Junior Web Site Evaluation
Computers with Internet access
Pencils

Directions:

1. Pre-load a Web site on the computers. Allow the screens to go to a screen saver or turn off the monitors so the students will not see the Web site when they arrive. For this evaluation I selected the Zoobooks site located at: http://www.zoobooks.com.
2. When the students arrive, begin the lesson by discussing the previous meeting's topic of book evaluation. Ask the students if they remember what some of the things are that they should look for when selecting a book. Discuss the type of information they would be looking for in a book and go over the Big 6 pizza wheel again.
3. Explain that today they are going to evaluate a Web site. Ask the students to think of what types of features they would evaluate in a Web site. Tell

the students that the Web site they will be looking at is about animals, the subject of their reports. Ask the students what type of information they think they will be looking for.

4. Have the students go to the computers and begin to look at the Web site. Ask the students to follow some of the links on the site and allow them to make their own navigation choices after showing the basics of the site. Give the students 15-20 minutes to navigate the site.
5. Hand out the *WebMAC Junior* evaluation forms and read the directions to the students. Explain how the form is similar to the one they filled out yesterday while evaluating the books.
6. Allow the students to continue to navigate the Web site while filling out the evaluation forms.
7. Once the students have completed the forms, collect them, and if time permits, score the forms for the students.
8. After the students have returned to class, complete the scoring of the forms and plot the group results on the chart provided.
9. Share the results of the evaluation with the students during the next meeting.
10. Share information about the project and the results with the teachers so they can continue to work on the topic of evaluation in the classrooms.

NOTE: *See Deb's reproducible instrument for books on the next page. She adapted it from our WebMAC Junior. It has a simpler scale (only three smiley faces) which makes it even easier for your youngest students. Although it doesn't include a scoring system like* WebMAC Junior, *it would be great for discussions and for teaching early evaluation skills for print-based resources.*

BookMAC

Adapted from WebMAC Junior (Arnone & Small, 1998) by Deb Christensen

Name: _____ Book Title: _____

Directions:

This is not a test. There are no right or wrong answers. This is a way to help you start looking at books and information to decide what is good or what needs to be improved. After reading each question, circle the face that best describes how you would rate this book.

EXAMPLE

If you circle the sad face, it means the book is **really poor in this area**. You give it the lowest score which is 0 points. If you circle the face with no expression (just a straight line for the mouth), it means the book is **OK, but there's nothing special about it**. If you circle the face with a smile, it means the book is **good or excellent**. You give it two points, the highest score.

1. When you first found this book, did it look like it would be interesting to read?

2. Did the information in the book seem believable and true?

3. Was there a lot of information in the book?

4. Would other students like this book?

5. Did you like the pictures or illustrations in the book?

6. Was the information you found in the book, or story, interesting to you?

7. Was this book fun to read?

8. Did you learn new things by reading this book?

9. How easy was it to find the information you needed?

10. Did the pictures make what you were reading more interesting?

11. Did this book make you feel like learning more about this subject or reading more books by this author?

Based on your experience with this book, please write below what you think are the best things about this book. Then write what you think could be improved about this book.

I think the "Best Things about This Book" are:

1. _____
2. _____
3. _____

I think the "Things that Need Improvement" are:

1. _____
2. _____
3. _____

Try to remember everything you can about this book. Overall, would you give this book an Up Arrow (like a "thumbs up") or a Down Arrow (like a "thumbs down")?

Up Arrow (good)   Down Arrow (poor)

What is your favorite book of all? _____

LESSON PLAN #2

Durhamville Elementary School by Linda Zuber

Lesson Name: Dewey Web Site and Evaluation

Class/Grade Level: Fifth

Instructional Goals:

▶ To reinforce and expand the students' understanding of the Dewey Decimal System.
▶ The students will understand that they can and should evaluate Web sites for accuracy, relevance, and ease of use.

Instructional Objectives:

▶ The students will be able to use the Dewey Web site to further their understanding of the Dewey Decimal System. The students will be able to use the Web site to answer questions on the question sheet.
▶ The students will come to the realization that those who use them should evaluate web sites for relevancy, authority and ease of use. The students will complete the *WebMAC Middle* form.

Motivation: Relevance—The students will view a Web site designed by students their age. The students will be given the chance to evaluate, thus offer their opinion of a Web site.

Procedure: The students will spend 15 minutes looking at the Web site by following directions and completing question sheet then complete the *WebMAC* evaluation sheet.

Materials/Resources: Web site "Do We" Really Know Dewey?
URL: http://tqjunior.advanced.org/5002/

Instructions for Students:
1. In Netscape, click on **Bookmarks—"Do We" Really Know Dewey?**
2. Write down the name and URL (or address) for this Web site on the front page of the *WebMAC Middle, Web Site Motivational Analysis Checklist* student booklet.

    The Web site name is: "Do We" Really Know Dewey?

The URL (or address) is: http://tqjunior.advanced.org/5002/

3. Read this Web page, then click on book at bottom right corner to find an explanation about why all books in the Dewey Classification System are not nonfiction.
4. Go back to the Dewey home page.
5. Click on the **Pre-Dew Review**. Explore these links by reading each page then clicking on the book at the bottom of the Web page to go to the next link. While you go through these Web pages you can answer questions 1–3 on the **Question Sheet**.
6. When you have reached **What does a NONFICTION call number look like?** click to go back to Dewey home on the icon located at the bottom right of the Web page.
7. If you still have time click on: **Let's "Dew" It**. From this page go to **General-to-Specific** and **Drop-Back Theory**. If you have time you can explore this entire Web site and look at anything that interests you. After you look at these pages you can answer question 4 and 5 on the **Question Sheet.**
8. Mrs. Zuber or Mrs. Carnevale will tell you when you can start completing the *WebMAC Middle*. Did you know that there are good and bad Web sites? There are many things we can look at to find out if a web site is good. Do you have a favorite TV show? Is your favorite TV show the same as your parents' or friends' favorite? Usually we have opinions about what we like and what we don't like. Now you will be able to give your opinion on this Web site. Remember when you fill out the *WebMAC* there are no right or wrong answers. You can look at this Web site while you fill out the form.

QUESTION SHEET

Answer these questions as you look at the "Do We" Really Know Dewey? Web site:

1. What kind of fiction books are located in the nonfiction section?

   _____

   _____

   _____

2. Dewey numbers always have how many numbers to the left of the decimal point? _____

3. Does a call number have to have a number ? _____

   Can you give an example? _____

4. What happens when you add more numbers to the Dewey Decimal number?

   _____

   _____

   _____

5. How can the Drop Back Theory help you get good information for a report?

   _____

   _____

   _____

Name _____

WEB PAGE ADDRESSES

example: http://www.oneidany.org/durham.htm

URL – The address of a web page. URL stands for uniform resource locator.

The URL for this example is: _____

Domain name – The domain identifies the electronic name of the location of the server. The domain name can consist of any combination of letters and numbers. Another term for this is host name.

The domain name for this example is: _____

Suffix – Identifies the type of organization operating the server. Common organizations are:

      .com   for companies
      .net   for networking companies
      .edu   for educational institutions
      .gov   for government departments and groups
      .mil   for military organizations
      .org   for organizations

The suffix name for this example is: _____

Think critically. Which of these types of organizations do you think would be most reliable for information? Which would be least reliable?

_____

_____

Tilde – A tilde looks like this: ~
When you see it on a Web address, it usually means that the Web page is a personal or business Web page on a server.

Think critically. Do you think information can be reliably factual on a personal Web page? Why or why not? Write your answer on the back of this sheet.

LESSON PLAN #3

West Point Elementary School by Kathy Sommers

Lesson Name: Black History Stamps

Class/Grade Level: Third Grade

Information Skills: Task definition, Information Use, Synthesis

Objectives:

- Students will compare information from two different sources.
- Students will evaluate information and select only those facts to meet a specified criterion.
- Students will use facts to support an opinion.
- (possibly) Students will recognize a need for more information.
- Students will evaluate Web site.

Resources:

- Encyclopedias
- Stamp on Black History Web site
  http://library.advanced.org/10320/Stamps.htm
- *WebMAC Junior*

Session 1
Materials:

- Commemorative stamps
- Note-taking sheet for each student
- OH transparency to model note-taking

Procedure:

1. LMS displays several commemorative stamps and asks students to speculate why appearing on stamps might honor people. It should be established that these people have done something significant.
2. LMS challenges students to solve some postal mysteries. Students will uncover facts about specific people who have appeared on commemorative stamps, trying to should look for facts that give reasons why their subject would merit such an honor. In other words, students are not looking for just any facts; they should find facts that clearly explain why this person

was chosen for a commemorative stamp.

3. LMS displays note-taking sheet OH and models fact-finding. Read articles from encyclopedia and Web site, stopping to ask whether students have heard any facts that would explain why subject is on a stamp. If so, students tell which source fact came from, and the LMS jots notes on OH and indicates source by checking appropriate columns.
4. Distribute note-taking worksheets. (Name of subject to be researched should be scan or cut-and-paste, attaching stamp to each note-taking sheet.)
5. LMS recommends sources to be used. To ensure student success, LMS should confirm that each research subject can be found in both the print and online sources. Students are to cite their two sources at top of sheet. Students should list several facts they feel are significant. Remind students to paraphrase—use their own words—when taking notes and check sources in appropriate column for each fact.
6. Stop about five minutes before end of session. Ask students to review their facts and make sure they have only written down facts that explain why this person may have been selected to be on a stamp. Students should place a star beside the most important reason they have listed.

Session 2

Prior to this session, LMS has assessed students' work to ensure each is ready for the next portion of the project. It may be necessary for some students to continue with Session 1 tasks.

Materials:

▶ Nomination applications
▶ OH transparency to model nominating
▶ Scrap paper for drafts of supporting paragraph

Procedure:

1. LMS announces that new stamps will be designed for use in the school's Wee Deliver mail system during Black History Month and proposes that students nominate for subject they researched last session. To alleviate concern that their subject might not be a strong candidate, emphasize that students' writing, rather than the person's accomplishments, will be the determining factor. To enter the competition, it will be necessary to submit an application form. Judges will review the entries and choose the most convincing suggestions. Briefly discuss attributes that might make judges favor one proposal over others. Stress need for specific facts rather than opinions to make the supporting paragraph (what the judges will look at) strong.

2. LMS models application form on OH, using starred fact on note-taking sheet "Most significant...." Other facts can be listed under "Accomplishments." These two sections should be combined to create the "Supporting paragraph."
3. Work together to fill out top portions of application, reviewing how to find birth/death dates and asking several students to share their one or two word descriptions.
4. Students complete "Most significant" and "Accomplishments" of the applications on their own. These sections are facts that can be used to create the supporting paragraph. They may refer back to the sources used last week and notes if necessary.

Students are to write a draft before writing the supporting paragraph on the application form. Remind them that a paragraph is a group of sentences about the same topic and should have a topic sentence to tie it together. The "Supporting paragraph" will be the only section at which the judges will look. Judges will consider this portion as the student's recommendation for their candidate. Make it clear that the strongest writing will be selected, rather than the actual achievements of the nominees.

Session 3
Materials:

▶ Application forms
▶ Optional: word searches, crossword puzzles, and so forth from Web site

Prior to this session, LMS has assessed students' work to ensure each is ready for next portion of project. It may be necessary for some students to continue with Session 2 tasks.

Procedure:

1. Students are to complete the nomination application form. Students may need to rewrite their draft, possibly referring back to notes from Session 1 and source. Remind students that judges will be looking only at the "Supporting paragraph" portion and may be influenced by neatness, correct spelling, and punctuation. They will definitely be persuaded by facts that explain why this person should be selected to appear on a stamp.
2. As students turn in applications, they may explore Web site alone or with partners to discover what other information and activities are available. LMS may have word searches, etc. from the Web site available for students to use to allow other students to get to computers to explore.
3. If time permits, group shares the variety of Web site activities they discovered while exploring.

Session 4

Materials:

▶ Winning nominations
▶ Blank 4" x 4" stamp forms

Prior to this session, selections have been made from among nominations. Judges chose "winners" who gave the clearest reasons why the nominee should be on a stamp. To design a stamp, artists will need information, not vague generalities, to convey in a visual format the accomplishments of the person selected.

LMS groups bios so that no winning entries are given to the class that will design a stamp for the chosen subject. As bios are passed out, ask whether anyone researched that person; if so, give that group a different paragraph.

Procedure:

1. LMS announces "winning" entries and provides one biography to each table. It may be necessary to explain that the LMS used the winning entries to prepare these paragraphs for this portion of the project. Some entries gave enough info, others needed two to be combined to provide enough facts for designers, others had (horrors!) incorrect info that the LMS has changed. Otherwise, student researchers have provided all information.
2. LMS provides general instructions for stamp entries: Designs should be appropriate representational symbols or scenes, not a portrait of the selected person such as were seen on the U.S. postage stamps. Images will be shrunk to stamp size, so designs need to be relatively large and mostly fill the 4" x 4" form. The name of the person must be on the stamp and will need to take up about one-fourth of the design so it will remain legible and being shrunk. Pencil is the best medium if there is no color copying capability; marks need to be dark to reproduce well.
3. Allow each group about five minutes to read biographies and discuss possible way to depict accomplishments for a stamp. LMS circulates, asking whether groups have any questions. When time is up, let students share any difficulties—did all groups feel they have adequate info to complete the task?
4. Then scramble students so that in each new group, each student is working on a different person. At any point in this or the previous step, students can use reference materials for additional info, if needed.
5. As students turn in stamp entries, return their nomination applications. Winning entrants are congratulated and asked what their nomination included that may account for their selection. Students whose nominations

were not selected are asked to review their forms and determine, if possible, why their nominee may not have been chosen.

Announcing winning nominations and stamp designs

LMS creates a sheet of stamps by reducing designs to stamp size and photocopies enough to distribute to all classrooms.

LMS sends a congratulatory note through Wee Deliver to inform those students whose information was used for bios and whose design is on stamps. Attach appropriate stamp to notes. Ask students to come to library and provide each with a first-day issue sheet of stamps (or announce in classrooms or over public address system).

Possible extensions:

▶ Have student winners complete a timeline display in the LMC by placing their entries in chronological order. LMS may wish to include information about the Springarn Medal and attach sticker/ribbon to any medal recipients among the winning entries.

▶ Create a PowerPoint presentation, which could be used for Open House or another appropriate setting.

Session 5 and later

Materials:

▶ *WebMAC Junior* evaluation instrument

Procedure:

1. LMS informs students about the *WebMAC Junior* evaluation instrument, relating that it can be useful in determining how useful, interesting, fun, or easy to navigate any Web site is. We will be rating the stamp on the Black History Web site. Students may be interested to learn that ThinkQuest, which is authored by groups of students and teachers, produces the site.
2. Class brainstorms favorable and weak features of Web site prior to filling out instrument.
   Possible example: Printout problems (wasted paper, did not print p.2...)
3. Students work in pairs to complete instrument. LMS reads each question; student must reach consensus on value to give each factor. They may need to defend strong opinions or may be willing to compromise if opinions differ.
4. LMS collects and tallies responses. At some later date, she explains in general terms how the instrument is structured, letting students

understand the meaning of the placement along each axis. Results of each class tally are displayed on OH transparency, significance of rating is explained. Discussion may follow. Tallies of other classes that participated in the valuation are also shared for comparison.

NOMINATION APPLICATION
for a new stamp

Details about the person:

Name: _____

Year of birth-Year of death: _____

One- or two-word description: _____

Accomplishments: _____

_____

_____

Most significant reason to consider this person for a stamp:

_____

_____

Supporting paragraph: _____

_____

_____

_____

_____

_____

_____

_____

_____

_____

Submitted by: _____

Name: _____ Class: _____

Source 1:

_____

_____

Source 2:

_____

_____

Source 1	FACTS	Source 2

Appendix C:
WebMAC Middle (2.0)

(Instrument, Score Sheets, Class Tally, and Plotting Grids)

WEBSITE MOTIVATIONAL ANALYSIS CHECKLIST
WebMAC Middle© (v.2.0)

WebMAC Middle is not a test. *There are no wrong answers.* It is a way of finding out what is good about this Web site and what needs to be improved. You are the judge.

Before using *WebMAC Middle*, it's a good idea to spend at least 20-30 minutes exploring the Web site to be evaluated in order to have some familiarity with its content and structure. You may need to go through the Web site at least once more to complete this checklist.

Rate your level of agreement with each of the 24 statements by placing the appropriate number value on the line in front of each item. If you are not sure about any item, select the best response you can give.

>**3** = I definitely agree.
>**2** = I mostly agree.
>**1** = I somewhat agree.
>**0** = I do NOT agree

Example of completed item:
-3- 0. This Web site makes me happy.

Read each question carefully. Think about your experience with this Web site before answering each question. If you need more help understanding how to use *WebMAC Middle*, ask your teacher for help.

Name_____ URL_____

WEBMAC MIDDLE (2.0)

3 = I definitely agree.
2 = I mostly agree.
1 = I somewhat agree.
0 = I do NOT agree

_____ 1. I like the colors and backgrounds used at this Web site.

_____ 2. This Web site is well-organized.

_____ 3. The information at this Web site is accurate and unbiased.

_____ 4. All the buttons and other mechanisms for moving around in this Web site work the way they should.

_____ 5. Something (such as a picture or title) on the home page of this Web site caught my attention.

_____ 6. I can read and understand most or all of the words at this Web site.

_____ 7. This Web site has connections (links) to other interesting or useful Web sites.

_____ 8. If I get lost or need help at this Web site, there are ways of getting help.

_____ 9. This Web site is fun and interesting to explore.

_____ 10. There is a menu or site map that helps me understand how much and what kinds of information I will find there.

_____ 11. All information at this Web site is related to the main topic.

_____ 12. I can control how fast I move through this Web site at all times.

_____ 13. There are surprising or unusual things at this Web site.

_____ 14. The purpose of this Web site is clear to me.

_____ 15. I find the information contained in this Web site to be current and up-to-date.

_____ 16. I do not need any special skills or experience to use this Web site.

_____ 17. The variety of formats (e.g., text, images, sound) keeps my attention.

WEBMAC MIDDLE (2.0)

3 = I definitely agree.
2 = I mostly agree.
1 = I somewhat agree.
0 = I do NOT agree

_____ 18. No matter where I am at this Web site I can return to the home page or exit.

_____ 19. The information at this Web site is useful to me.

_____ 20. All of the Web site's links work the way they should.

_____ 21. This Web site has unusual or unique features that make it more interesting.

_____ 22. There is enough of what I am interested in (or looking for) on this Web site.

_____ 23. There is a way to communicate with the author of this Web site.

_____ 24. At all times, I can control what information at this Web site I wish to see.

Now, you are ready to answer the final questions.

This is a Web site I would like to visit again at another time.   YES ☐   No ☐

This is a Web site that friends my age would like to visit.   YES ☐   No ☐

Based on your experience with this Web site, please write below what you think are the best things about this Web site. Then, write what you think could be improved about this Web site.

"Best Things About This Web site"

a.) _____

b.) _____

c.) _____

WEBMAC MIDDLE (2.0)

"Things That Need Improvement"

a.) _____

b.) _____

c.) _____

Overall, would you give this Web site a **thumbs up** or a **thumbs down**? Circle your answer. (If you just can't make up your mind, then circle the person who is scratching his head.)

Gets my vote!   Undecided   Needs lots of improvement!

Wait for instructions from your teacher or library media specialist before scoring.

SCORING WebMAC MIDDLE (2.0)

After completing the questionnaire, use this sheet to copy your score for each question next to the number of that question. Notice that odd-numbered questions are under column **A** and even-numbered questions are under column **B**.

A	**B**
1. _____	2. _____
3. _____	4. _____
5. _____	6. _____
7. _____	8. _____
9. _____	10. _____
11. _____	12. _____
13. _____	14. _____
15. _____	16. _____
17. _____	18. _____
19. _____	20. _____
21. _____	22. _____
23. _____	24. _____

TOTAL
A Scores _____

TOTAL
B Scores _____

UNDERSTANDING YOUR SCORES

The "<u>A</u>" score represents how interesting or useful you feel this Web site is. A low score indicates that you don't feel it has much to offer to you personally. The "<u>B</u>" score refers to how well the Web site works. This covers things like how easy or difficult it was to find your way around, how well the designer did his or her job of making sure everything works correctly, and how clear and organized the information was. A low score here, for example, means that you did not feel confident that you could easily find your way around or get the information you needed. Once you have scored *WebMAC Middle*, you can refer to the score key below to see how well the Web site rated. A Web site that gets high scores in both <u>A</u> and <u>B</u> is an ***Awesome Web Site!***

SCORE KEY

<u>A</u> *(How Interesting)*   <u>B</u> *(How Well It Worked)*

    0 – 9 Poor   0 – 9 Poor
    10 – 17 Below Average   10 – 17 Below Average
    18 – 24 Average   18 – 24 Average
    25 – 30 Good   25 – 30 Good
    31 – 36 Outstanding   31 – 36 Outstanding

Outstanding <u>A</u> + Outstanding <u>B</u> = ***Awesome Web Site!***

RATING THIS WEB SITE: STUDENT

DIRECTIONS: On the plotting grid, you will notice that the horizontal line is for the "How Interesting" score (the **A** score) and the vertical line is for the "How Well It Works" score (the **B** score). Place a dot for the **A** score along the *Not Interesting – Very Interesting* line; place a dot for the **B** score along the *Works Well – Works Poorly* line. Then, draw straight lines to their point of intersection (where the lines cross). Good Web sites will have both scores in the upper right section. An awesome Web site will have scores that fall in the extreme upper right section.

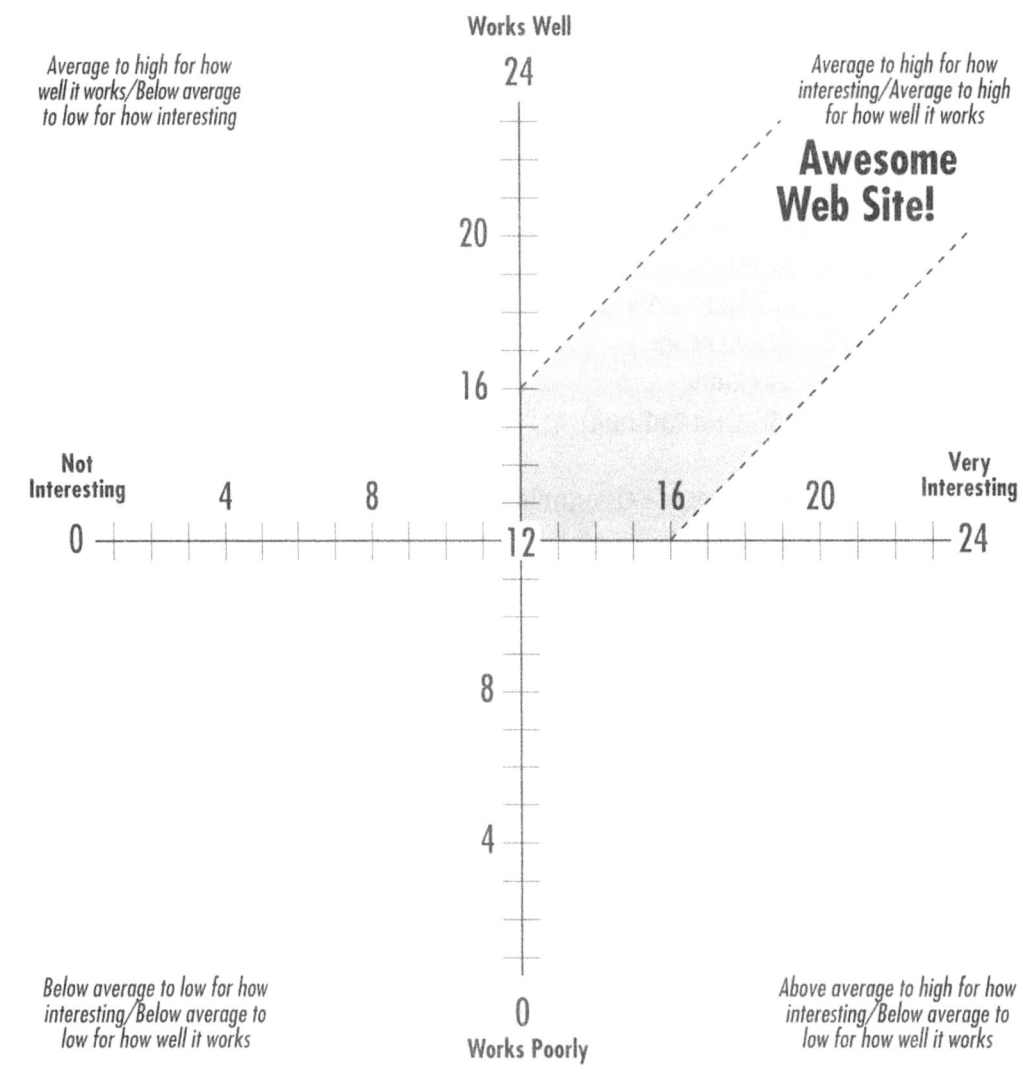

CLASS TALLY

INSTRUCTOR DIRECTIONS: If you would like your class to see a summary and an average of all the individual total scores, use the tally sheet below (for class size up to 30 students) to record individual total scores for **A** and **B**. Then, average each list. Later, you will plot the class average scores for **A** and **B** on the class grid. (Use this class tally sheet only after each student has finished his or her individual questionnaire.)

A	**B**
1. _____	1. _____
2. _____	2. _____
3. _____	3. _____
4. _____	4. _____
5. _____	5. _____
6. _____	6. _____
7. _____	7. _____
8. _____	8. _____
9. _____	9. _____
10. _____	10. _____
11. _____	11. _____
12. _____	12. _____
13. _____	13. _____
14. _____	14. _____
15. _____	15. _____
16. _____	16. _____
17. _____	17. _____
18. _____	18. _____
19. _____	19. _____
20. _____	20. _____
21. _____	21. _____
22. _____	22. _____
23. _____	23. _____
24. _____	24. _____
25. _____	25. _____
26. _____	26. _____
27. _____	27. _____
28. _____	28. _____
29. _____	29. _____
30. _____	30. _____

Total A Scores: _____   **Total B Scores:** _____

Average A Scores: _____   Average B Scores: _____

RATING THIS WEB SITE: CLASS

INSTRUCTOR DIRECTIONS: Use the results of the class tally sheet and plot the average **A** score (Value or *How Interesting*) and **B** score (Expectation for Success or *How Well It Works*) on the grid below.

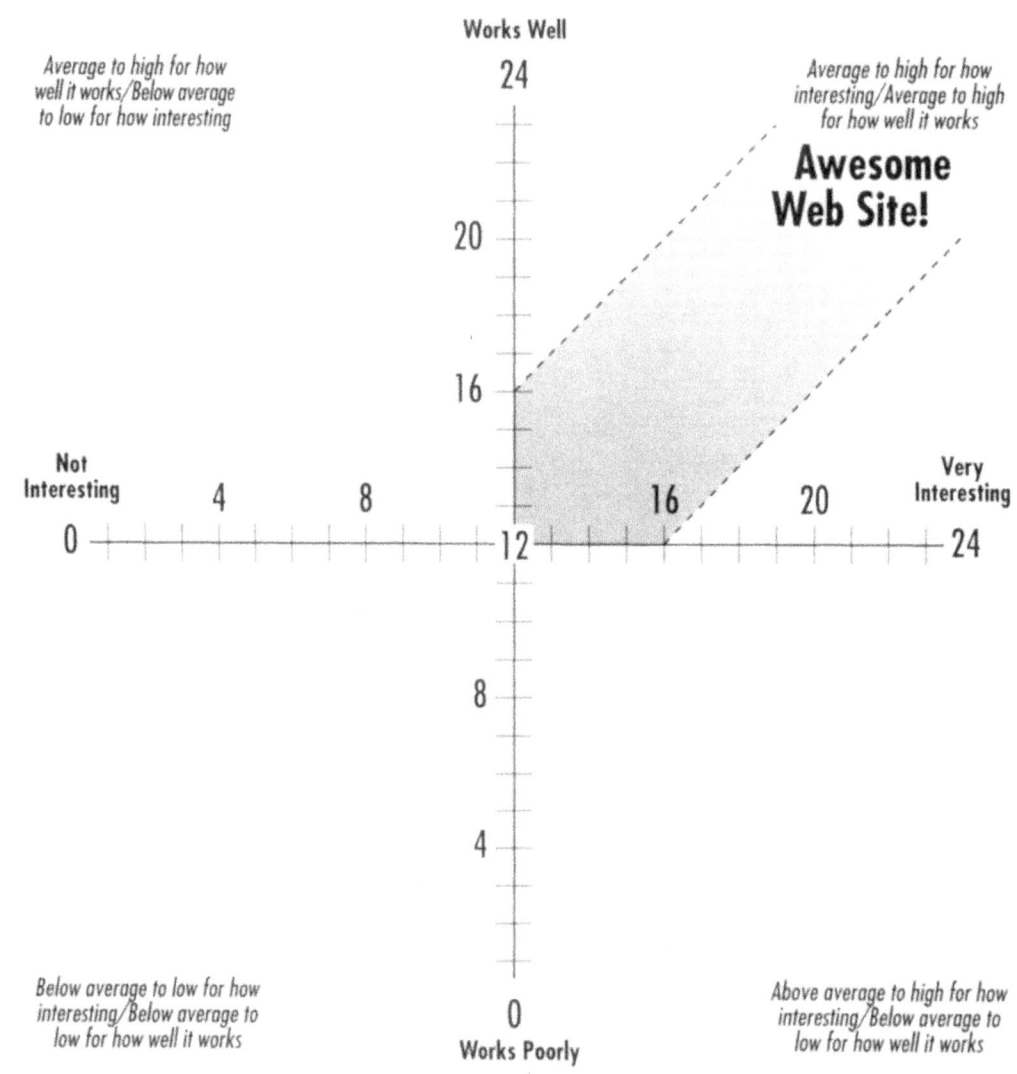

Appendix D:
WebMAC Junior Long Form

(Instrument, Score Sheets, Class Tally, and Plotting Grids)

WebMAC Junior Long Form

(©1999, Marilyn P. Arnone, Ph.D. & Ruth V. Small, Ph.D.)

Name: _____ School: _____

Grade: _____ Date: _____

Web Site Address: _____

Instructions

Just like the judges who decide the winners in an art or science contest, you are one of the judges for this Web site. After reading each question, circle the face that best describes how you would rate this Web site. Remember that ***there are no right or wrong answers***. First, try the example below.

Example

Did this Web site contain things that you are interested in?

If you circle the <u>sad face</u> ☹, it means that this Web site is really poor in this category. In other words, there is nothing in this Web site that is of interest to you. You give it the lowest score, which is 0 points. If you circle the face with <u>no expression</u> 😐 (just a straight line for the mouth), it means that this Web site is OK, but there's nothing special that interests you. If you circle the face with a <u>small smile</u> 🙂, it means that this Web site is not the best, but it is good. If you circle the face with a <u>big smile</u> 😊, it means that this Web site is excellent—definitely one of the best Web sites you have seen when it comes to things that interest you. You give it 3 points, the highest score.

WebMAC Junior Long Form 4.0

1. Was this an interesting or fun Web site to explore?

2. Could you read and understand most of the words that were used?

3. Was the information at this Web site believable? (Did it seem to be true?)

4. Was it easy to find your way around without getting lost?

5. Did the pictures, sounds, or videos make this Web site more interesting?

6. Was it easy to find what you needed at this Web site?

7. Did this Web site have links to other interesting or useful Web sites?

　　　😦　😐　🙂　😃
　　　0　　1　　2　　3

8. Did all the parts of this Web site work the way they should?

　　　😦　😐　🙂　😃
　　　0　　1　　2　　3

9. Were there lots of activities to do at this Web site?

　　　😦　😐　🙂　😃
　　　0　　1　　2　　3

10. Were the directions for using this Web site simple and clear?

　　　😦　😐　🙂　😃
　　　0　　1　　2　　3

11. Do you think this Web site sometimes adds new things to read about and do?

　　　😦　😐　🙂　😃
　　　0　　1　　2　　3

12. Did things like pictures, games, or videos *quickly* come up on the screen?

　　　😦　😐　🙂　😃
　　　0　　1　　2　　3

13. Did you like the colors and backgrounds used at this Web site?

　　　😦　😐　🙂　😃
　　　0　　1　　2　　3

14. Did you find *enough* of what you were looking for at this Web site?

15. Was what you found at this Web site useful to you?

16. Were there ways of getting help if you needed it at this Web site?

17. Were there any surprising or unusual things at this Web site?

18. When you first arrived, was it clear what this Web site was all about?

19. Did you learn new things by visiting this Web site?

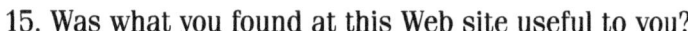

20. Could you easily control what you wanted to do and see at this Web site?

21. Was there enough going on at this Web site to keep your attention?

☹ 😐 🙂 😊
0   1   2   3

22. Wherever you were, could you always return to the home page or exit?

☹ 😐 🙂 😊
0   1   2   3

23. Did this Web site make you feel like learning more about this topic?

☹ 😐 🙂 😊
0   1   2   3

24. Were the pictures, cartoons, or videos clear and easy to see?

☹ 😐 🙂 😊
0   1   2   3

Would you like to visit this Web site again sometime? (✔) YES ☐ NO ☐

Is this a Web site that friends your age would like to visit? YES ☐ NO ☐

What did you like **best** about this Web site? Write in the space below.

_____

_____

_____

What would make this Web site **better**? Write your ideas below.

_____

_____

_____

Now, YOU be the judge! Overall, would you give this Web site a **_thumbs up_** or a **_thumbs down_**? Circle your answer. (If you just can't make up your mind, then circle the person who is scratching his head.)

Gets my vote!	Undecided	Needs lots of improvement!

SCORING *WebMAC JUNIOR* (4.0)

After listening to the directions, place your score for each question next to the number of that question. Notice that odd-numbered questions are under column **A** and even-numbered questions are under column **B**.

<u>**A**</u>   <u>**B**</u>

1. _____   2. _____
3. _____   4. _____
5. _____   6. _____
7. _____   8. _____
9. _____   10. _____
11. _____   12. _____
13. _____   14. _____
15. _____   16. _____
17. _____   18. _____
19. _____   20. _____
21. _____   22. _____
23. _____   24. _____

TOTAL   **TOTAL**
A Scores _____   **B Scores** _____

UNDERSTANDING YOUR SCORES

The "**A**" score represents how interesting or useful you feel this Web site is. A low score indicates that you don't feel it has much to offer to you personally. The "**B**" score refers to how well the Web site works. This covers things like how easy or difficult it was to find your way around, how well the designer did his or her job of making sure everything works correctly, and how clear and organized the information was. A low score here, for example, means that you did not feel confident that you could easily find your way around or get the information you needed. Once you have scored *WebMAC Junior*, you can refer to the score key below to see how well the Web site rated. A Web site that gets high scores in both **A** and **B** is an ***Awesome Web Site***!

SCORE KEY

A *(How Interesting)*
- 0 – 9 Poor
- 10 – 17 Below Average
- 18 – 24 Average
- 25 – 30 Good
- 31 – 36 Outstanding

B *(How Well It Worked)*
- 0 – 9 Poor
- 10 – 17 Below Average
- 18 – 24 Average
- 25 – 30 Good
- 31 – 36 Outstanding

Outstanding **A** + Outstanding **B** = ***Awesome Web Site!***

RATING THIS WEB SITE: STUDENT

DIRECTIONS: On the plotting grid, you will notice that the horizontal line is for the "How Interesting" score (the **A** score) and the vertical line is for the "How Well It Works" score (the **B** score). Place a dot for the **A** score along the *Not Interesting – Very Interesting* line; place a dot for the **B** score along the *Works Well – Works Poorly* line. Then, draw straight lines to their point of intersection (where the lines cross). Good Web sites will have both scores in the upper right section. An awesome Web site will have scores that fall in the extreme upper right section.

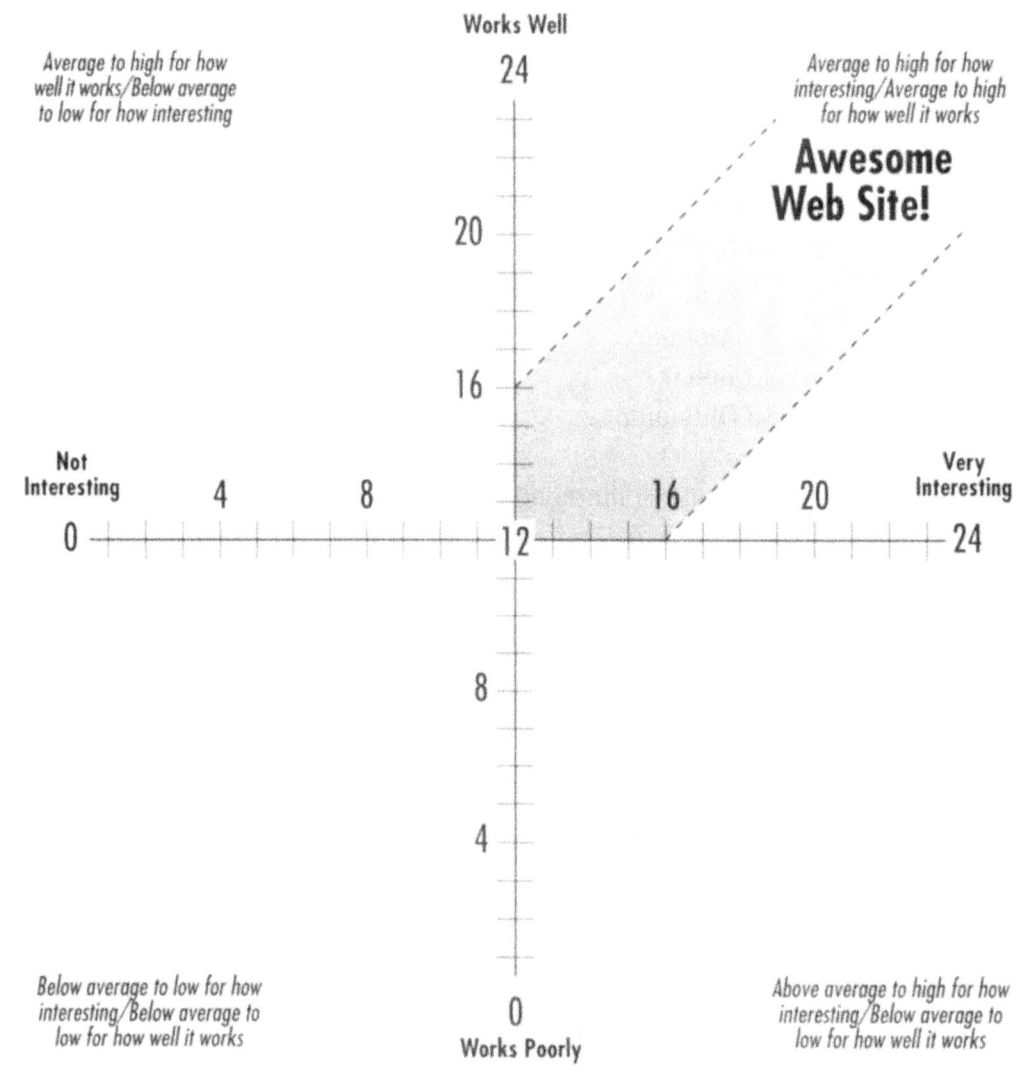

CLASS TALLY

INSTRUCTOR DIRECTIONS: If you would like your class to see a summary and an average of all the individual total scores, use the tally sheet below to record individual total scores for **A** and **B**. Then, average each list. Later, you will plot the class average scores for **A** and **B** on the grid provided.

A	**B**
1. _____	1. _____
2. _____	2. _____
3. _____	3. _____
4. _____	4. _____
5. _____	5. _____
6. _____	6. _____
7. _____	7. _____
8. _____	8. _____
9. _____	9. _____
10. _____	10. _____
11. _____	11. _____
12. _____	12. _____
13. _____	13. _____
14. _____	14. _____
15. _____	15. _____
16. _____	16. _____
17. _____	17. _____
18. _____	18. _____
19. _____	19. _____
20. _____	20. _____
21. _____	21. _____
22. _____	22. _____
23. _____	23. _____
24. _____	24. _____
25. _____	25. _____
26. _____	26. _____
27. _____	27. _____
28. _____	28. _____
29. _____	29. _____
30. _____	30. _____

Total A Scores: _____   **Total B Scores:** _____

Average A Scores: _____   Average B Scores: _____

RATING THIS WEB SITE: CLASS

INSTRUCTOR DIRECTIONS: Use the results of the class tally sheet and plot the average **A** score (Value or *How Interesting*) and **B** score (Expectation for Success or *How Well It Works*) on the grid below.

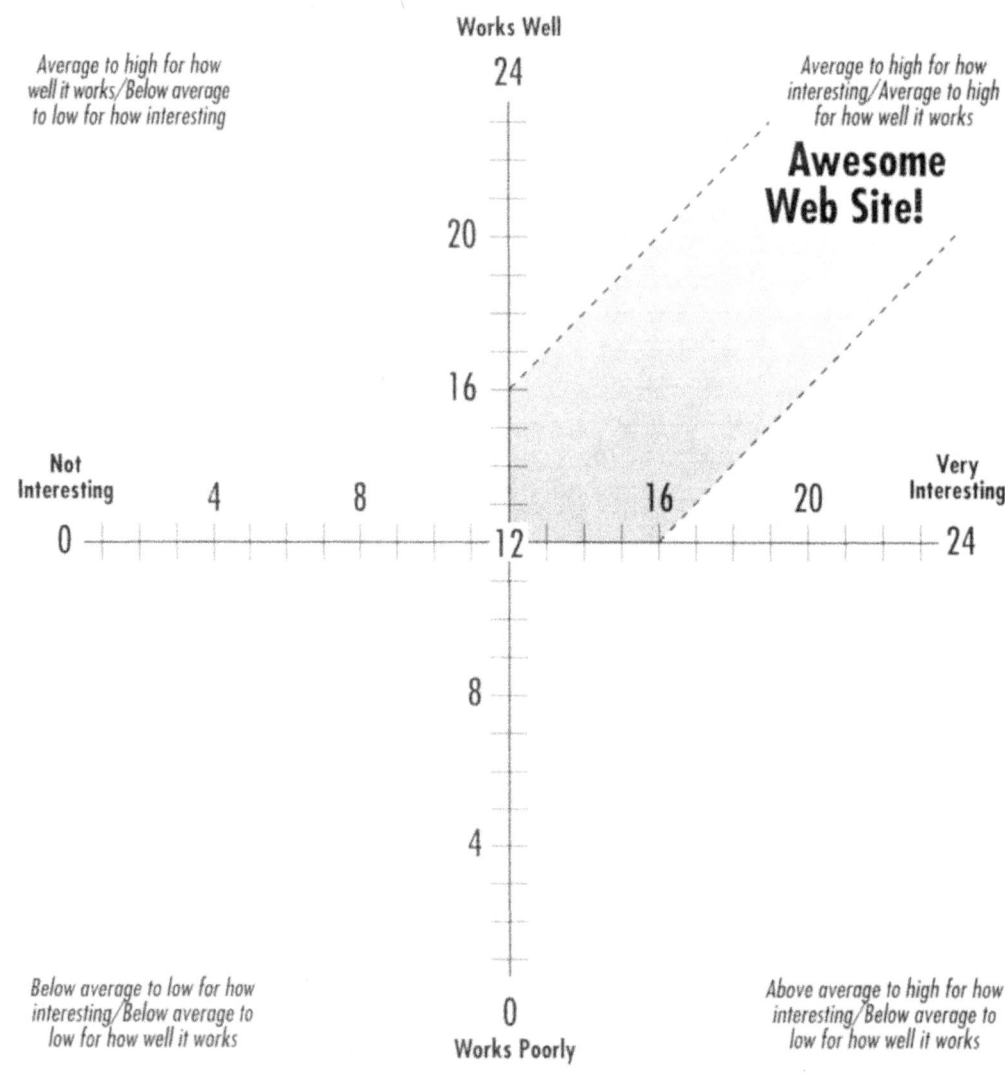

Appendix E:
Web Site Investigator

INVESTIGATOR (2.0)

Name: _____ School: _____

Grade: _____ Date: _____

Web Site Address: _____

Instructions

As a Web Site Investigator, you can check out Web sites for clues that tell you whether a Web site is a good one, an OK one, or a poor one. Good Web sites are interesting and useful. They stay up-to-date and add new things often. A good Web site has information you can trust. You can look for clues about who wrote the information on the Web site. A good Web site also works the way it should without broken links or games that don't even load. It should also be fun to explore and easy to find your way around. Awesome Web sites are the ones that are good in all these things. Are you ready to snoop around for clues about the Web site you are going to rate? If you are, read the example and then get to work. By the way, there are no right or wrong answers. That's because it is really up to what you think as a Web Site Investigator.

Example

Did this Web site contain things that you are interested in?

If you circle the sad face ☹, it means that this Web site is really poor in this category. In other words, there is nothing in this Web site that is of interest to you. You give it the lowest score, which is 0 points. If you circle the face with no expression 😐 (just a straight line for the mouth), it means that this Web site is OK, but there's nothing special that interests you. If you circle the face with a small smile 🙂, it means that this Web site is not the best, but it is good. If you circle the face with a big smile 😃, it means that this Web site is excellent—definitely one of the best Web sites you have seen when it comes to things that interest you. You give it 3 points, the highest score.

WEB SITE INVESTIGATOR (2.0)

Investigator's Name: _____

Web Site Address: _____

1. Was this an interesting or fun Web site to explore?

2. Could you read and understand most of the words that were used?

3. Was the information on this Web site believable? (Did it seem to be true?)

4. Was it easy to find your way around without getting lost?

5. Did the pictures, sounds, or videos make this Web site more interesting?

6. Was it easy to find what you needed at this Web site?

7. Did this Web site have links to other interesting or useful Web sites?

   0   1   2   3

8. Did all the parts of this Web site work the way they should?

   0   1   2   3

9. Were there lots of activities to do on this Web site?

   0   1   2   3

10. Were the directions for using this Web site simple and clear?

    0   1   2   3

11. Do you think this Web site sometimes adds new things to read about and do?

    0   1   2   3

12. Did things like pictures, games, and videos quickly come up on screen?

    0   1   2   3

Would you like to visit this Web site again sometime? (✔)   YES ☐   NO ☐

Do you think other kids your age would like this Web site?   YES ☐   NO ☐

SCORING *WEB SITE INVESTIGATOR*

DIRECTIONS: Add up the scores for each question. Then, use the scoring key below to see how you rated this Web site.

Score	Rating
33 or more points	Awesome!
28 – 32	Good
23 – 26	Average
22 and under	Needs improvement!

Index

Index

A

accuracy of information, 23, 104, 161, 188.
ARCS Model of Motivational Design, 20.
Ask-an-Expert services, 7-8.
authenticity of information, 22, 188.
authority of Web site, 22, 85, 104, 115, 188, 201.
Awesome Web Site Award (AWArd), 110, 177.

B

bias, author's, 22, 188-189.
Big6 Model of Information Problem-Solving, 4, 5-6.
BookMAC, 101, 195-97.

C

clarity of Web site, 23.
comprehensive coverage, 23, 188.
content validity, 22, 23, 85, 104, 133, 188.
Critical Evaluation Survey, 41-42.
currency, 10-11, 22, 23, 161, 189.
Cyberguides, 41.

D

data mining, 21.
digital literacy, 10.
domain names (as authority clues), 11.

E

evaluation of Web sites, 5-6, 10-11, 58, 98, 104-106, 115, 124-25, 132-33, 160-61, 164.
Expectancy-Value (E-V) Theory, 19-21, 23, 133, 139-40;
    applying to Web sites, 24-28, 42;
    and *WebMAC*, 42-45, 77, 84-86.
expectation for success, 19-21, 23-24, 25, 27, 133-134, 142, 146.

F

FLIP-IT Model, 4.
functionality of Web site, effect on motivation, 23, 24-28, 85-86.

I

information literacy, 4-6.
Internet:
    basic terminology, 58-59, 161, 165, 201;
    use as teaching tool, 6-10, 96-110.
intrinsic motivation, 18.

L

Library Selection Criteria for WWW Resources, 41.

M

Model of the Search Process, 4.
motivation:
    importance of, 18;
    strategies for improving, 97, 99-100.
motivation mining, 21, 133, 137-38.
motivational quality of Web sites, 18, 20-23, 133-34, 140-44.
Multimedia Schools, 7.

O

overheads for use with *WebMAC Junior*, 160-162;
    masters, 136-51, 163-76.

P

Pathways to Knowledge: Follett Information Skills Model, 4, 6.

R

Research Process Model, 4.

S

student perceptions, 21, 22-23, 24, 96-110.
Super Three, 6.

T

Taxonomy of Educational Objectives, 5.
teacher judgments, 21, 22, 24, 51-52, 114-15.
terminology, Internet, 58-59, 161, 165, 201.
Thinking Critically About World Wide Web Resources, 41.
tools, for Web evaluation, 40-44, 134, 147-48;
    See also specific tools.
TSA Model for Web-Based Instruction, 22-24;
    See also student perceptions;
        teacher judgments;
        Web site attributes.

V

value, 19-21, 23-24, 25-26, 27, 133-34, 145, 142.

W

Web resources, examples, 7-9.
Web site attributes, 21-22.
Web Site Investigator, 234-37.
Web Site Motivational Analysis Checklist (WebMAC), 40, 42-45, 134, 147-48;
    development of, 45-50;
    other instruments, 45, 117;
    as lesson planning tool, 51-52, 114-15, 134;
    as research and development tool, 52-53, 66, 116-19, 134;
    as teaching tool, 50-51, 96-110, 118, 134;
    See also WebMAC Junior;
        WebMAC Middle.
WebMAC Junior, 40, 43-44, 46-50, 67-70, 74-80, 134, 147-51, 161;
    administration of, 48, 58-61;
    in-service workshop, 132-56;
    interpretation of, 84-87, 162, 174;
    lesson plans using, 192-209;
    Long Form, 45, 46-47, 222-32;
    scoring, 74-80, 162;
    uses of, 96-110, 125;
    See also Web Site Motivational Analysis Checklist (WebMAC);
        WebMAC Middle.
WebMAC Middle, 44-45, 66, 115, 117-18, 135, 198-99, 212-20;
    See also Web Site Motivational Analysis Checklist (WebMAC);
        WebMAC Middle.

www.ingramcontent.com/pod-product-compliance
Lightning Source LLC
Chambersburg PA
CBHW080409300426
44113CB00015B/2455